MW00633959

THE LEVANTINE VEGETARIAN

SALMA HAGE

THE LEVANTINE VEGETARIAN

RECIPES FROM THE MIDDLE EAST

Φ

LEGEND 007
INTRODUCTION 008

SNACKS 010
SMALL PLATES 026
SALADS 054
SANDWICHES 076
BRUNCH 094
SOUPS & STEWS 112
RICE & GRAINS 130
VEGETABLES 154
BREADS 192
DESSERTS 214
DRINKS 238
SPICES, SAUCES & PRESERVES 250

INDEX 262
RECIPE NOTES 272

LEGEND

- VE Vegan
- DF Dairy-free
- GF Gluten-free
- NF Nut-free
- 30 30 minutes or less
- 5 5 ingredients or fewer

INTRODUCTION

The Levant refers to a large, approximate geographical region. The Levantine countries are historically coastal, taking in the Eastern Mediterranean shores, and include Syria, Lebanon, Israel, Palestine, Jordan and parts of Egypt and Turkey. Crudely, the Levant sits within the Middle East. These fertile lands have a wealth of agricultural history, with some of the world's earliest farmers cultivating grain, cereals, fresh fruits and vegetables, and facilitating trade between Asia and Europe thousands of years ago.

The standard Levantine menu is so vibrant and varied, with herby tabbouleh, enticing creamy dips like walnut muhammara, and mainstays baba ghanoush and hummus as certain as the salt and paper napkins on the tables. Indeed, the countries that make up the Levant share many of the same iconic dishes. In fact, at home, and in cafes and restaurants, these dishes have many variations, with changes in the use of spice and cookery techniques. Although not historically a 'vegetarian' region, meat represented special occasions and times of celebration and feasting, so for most families, mealtimes were and are by necessity made up of vegetarian or vegan dishes.

The wonderful recipes from the Levant naturally lend themselves to sharing. Mezze feasts that begin with smoky eggplant (aubergine) mutabel and creamy hummus, ready to be scooped up with steaming, pillowy flatbreads; and textured salads, made with the best of this season's fresh vegetables and last season's harvest, pickled and preserved to a tangy crunch, are the embodiment of generous hosting and happy eating. Modern lifestyles can mean that hours-long meals of little sharing dishes are often impractical, and lunch or dinner will more likely consist of a flatbread wrap or stew alongside bread or rice. In this book, you'll find ideas for both leisurely meals to share, as well as midweek dinners when you need to get a sustaining and nutritious supper on the table quickly.

Until fairly recently, many, if not most, in this region cooked using portable braziers and communal ovens for breads, and then, when the fierce heat died down, soaked grains and pulses would turn plump and tender in the residual heat left by the dying embers. Technological advances and changes in lifestyle have altered the way families, young professionals and different generations cook and eat in the Levant, with the same interests in trends and healthy lifestyle choices as we have in the West. In many cases, this has made traditional recipes more accessible, but culinary traditions evolve, and the dishes from the Levant are familiar across the map, but with many variations, and a loose approach to precise measurements and techniques. Fruits and vegetables come in different sizes, while the soil and access to direct sunlight that these products of nature have will be different, and for that reason I encourage you to taste as you go, and to feel liberated to tweak and personalise my recipes to suit your tastes.

The enduring heritage of these recipes is aided by the fact that they are incidentally healthy (often vegan), and based around wholefoods like pulses, fresh vegetables and verdant herbs. As more people around the world adopt vegan and vegetarian diets, there's an appetite for ingredients and recipes that provide richness and protein, without meat replacements or dietary supplements. Little wonder, then, that recipes from the Levant like crisp and gently spicy falafel, and creamy lentil stews, lifted with a bright spritz of lemon or sumac, have become mainstays on menus from New York to Sydney. These dishes naturally offer a rich library of flavours and are balanced with protein and fibre by virtue of the pulses, grains, vegetables and condiments that make up the culinary repertoire of the region.

Undoubtedly, the quality of produce makes the difference between a good and bad dining experience, particularly when fresh vegetables are pickled to add an element of crunch, or bright green herbs are part of the dish to bring freshness and balance. There's a saying in my house, though: 'spice is where the flavour comes from'. So many of the best meals I've had are because whoever is cooking has an instinctive understanding of how and when to use spice to utmost effect. Whether earthy cumin is added to chickpea stews to bring a complex warmth, or whole spices are tempered in sizzling hot oil, so that when you eat the food they're drizzled on it is as though you're eating the distilled essence of that flavour, spices create the complexity and intrigue. There isn't enough room to write a history of the spice trade in the Levantine region here, but what is commonly known is that spice traders were peddling pepper and cinnamon throughout the region as early as 2000 BC. Spices were held with as much import as precious stones and textiles, and so the trade developed from India to transport the spices over land rather than via sea to prevent spoilage. These days, spices are available in every supermarket and corner shop, although some, such as Iranian saffron (the best you can buy, in my opinion), is more expensive today than gold, because harvesting it is so laborious. Thank goodness, then, that a little goes a long way, as you'll see if you cook my Celebration Pie (page 191).

While the region has enjoyed periods of prosperity, its people have suffered from ongoing political unrest, corruption, invasion and religious disagreement, although conflict today is as much about land, access to natural resources and rights as it is about religion. With conflict, tragically, comes displacement of people from their homes, but this could be one reason why some of the foods of the Levant are so ubiquitous across the region. In every country in the area, you'll find different takes on falafel, hummus and rice. There are some food traditions, however, that are specific to certain countries, cities and chefs. Throughout this book, you'll find common dishes you might expect to find from a shop front or cart in Lebanon, Israel or Jordan, but I hope to also introduce you to new dishes, such as a Palestinian Musakhan (page 166).

From Turkey to Egypt, the recipes in this book are a collection of culinary links that bind the Levantine region together – modern twists on classics and exotic flavours brought to the region by travellers and traders from faraway lands. Above all, this food is accessible, inclusive and informal – it will leave you craving more. I hope you enjoy cooking these dishes and sharing them in your kitchen as much as I enjoyed creating them.

—Salma Hage

SNACKS

L–R Beetroot Muhammara (page 16), Garlic Walnut Dip (page 16), Za'atar Fries (page 23), Roasted Carrot Mezze (page 180).

AUBERGINE FRIES

Serves 4 as a mezze

- 1 large aubergine (eggplant), cut into long batons, about 1 cm/½ inch thick
- 500 ml/17 fl oz (2 cups plus 1 tablespoon) milk or nut milk
- Vegetable or sunflower oil, for frying
- 75 g/2¾ oz (generous ½ cup) fine ground polenta
- 75 g/2¾ oz (scant ¾ cup) cornflour (cornstarch)
- ½ teaspoon cayenne pepper
- Salt and black pepper
- 3 tablespoons grape molasses
- Flaky sea salt, for finishing

Crispy on the outside and meltingly tender on the inside, these fries make an enjoyable pre-dinner snack when served with an ice-cold drink.

Grape molasses is vital to this dish. Track it down at Middle Eastern shops or online.

In a large bowl, combine the aubergine (eggplant) and milk. Using a small plate, press down so that the aubergine is submerged in the milk. Set aside for at least 45 minutes.

Heat the oil in a large frying pan or skillet to a depth of at least 5 mm/¼ inch over medium heat. Drain the aubergine and discard the liquid. Pat dry with paper towels. Set aside.

Combine the polenta, cornflour (cornstarch), cayenne pepper and a generous pinch of salt and pepper in a large bowl. Mix well. Add the aubergine and toss thoroughly to coat.

Working in batches, lower the aubergine into the oil and fry for 5–7 minutes, until golden all over. Using a slotted spoon, transfer the aubergines to a paper towel-lined plate. Repeat with the remaining aubergine, adding more oil when the pan looks dry.

Immediately drizzle with the grape molasses and sprinkle with the flaky sea salt. Serve warm.

SPICY ROASTED CHICKPEAS

Serves 2

- 1 x (400-g/14-oz) can chickpeas
- 2 teaspoons ground cumin
- 1 teaspoon hot smoked paprika
- 1 teaspoon ground coriander
- ¼ teaspoon ground cinnamon
- ¼ teaspoon cayenne pepper
- Large pinch of salt
- 1 tablespoon light olive oil

Growing up in Lebanon, I'd enjoy piping hot, freshly roasted chickpeas in paper cones, a crunchy and spicy treat whenever our family would go into town. In the UK, it's not easy to find fresh chickpeas, so I make a version with readily available canned chickpeas and spices.

Eat these as you would roast nuts, or sprinkle them over salads for pops of flavour.

Preheat the oven to 200°C/400°F/Gas Mark 6. Drain the chickpeas and pat dry on paper towels.

In a bowl, combine all the ingredients and toss until the chickpeas are coated. Transfer the chickpeas to a baking sheet and roast for 35 minutes, tossing halfway, until golden and crispy. Set aside to cool.

Leftover roasted chickpeas can be stored in an airtight container for up to 3 days.

BEETROOT MUHAMMARA

Serves 4–6 as a starter or mezze

400 g/14 oz beetroot (beets), unpeeled and scrubbed
75 g/2¾ oz (⅔ cup) toasted walnuts
4 tablespoons extra-virgin olive oil, plus extra for drizzling
1 teaspoon cumin seeds, toasted
1 large garlic clove, peeled
1 tablespoon Pomegranate Molasses (page 256)
1 teaspoon red wine vinegar
½ teaspoon sumac
3 tablespoons dill sprigs
Salt and black pepper
50 g/1¾ oz crumbled feta (optional)
Lebanese Flatbreads (page 198) or crudités, to serve

***Muhammara* is the Arabic word for 'reddened', hence the name of this traditional dip made with red peppers and red pepper flakes. This beetroot (beet) version is something I prepare regularly – an earthy, and extremely healthy, standby in the refrigerator for a quick lunch or pre-dinner dip.**

Place the beetroots (beets) in a large saucepan and fill with enough cold water to cover by at least 2 cm/¾ inch. Bring to a boil, then reduce the heat to medium-low and simmer for 1–1½ hours, until the beetroots are completely tender. Drain, then steam dry.

When cool enough to handle, rub the skins off the beetroots. Use gloves to prevent your hands from staining. Discard the skins, then roughly chop the beetroots and transfer to a food processor with the remaining ingredients, except the sumac and dill. Season with 1 teaspoon salt and a generous grind of pepper. Blitz until a smooth paste forms. Season to taste with more vinegar or salt.

Using a rubber spatula, transfer the muhammara to a serving bowl, then top with a generous drizzle of olive oil, the sumac and dill. Add the crumbled feta, if using. Serve at room temperature with grilled flatbreads or crudités.

The muhammara can be stored in an airtight container in the refrigerator for up to 5 days.

GARLIC AND WALNUT DIP

Serves 4–6

2 slices stale white bread (50 g/1¾ oz)
3 tablespoons extra-virgin olive oil, plus extra for drizzling
1 tablespoon lemon juice
1 teaspoon red wine vinegar
2 garlic cloves, crushed
75 g/2¾ oz (⅔ cup) toasted walnuts
¾ teaspoon salt
¼ teaspoon ground cumin
¼ teaspoon cayenne pepper
¼ teaspoon ground coriander
2 tablespoons tahini
Sprig of parsley, finely chopped
Lebanese Flatbreads (page 198) and pickles, to serve

Depending on where you land, this dip (*tarator*) means different things to different people. In northern Turkey, it's a dill and yogurt affair, punctuated with cooling cucumber. In Syria, it's a rich tahini dip. My favourite is this walnut version which is wonderful with crudités, in sandwiches or as an accompaniment to grilled vegetables, fish and meats.

Place the bread in a bowl and cover with cold water. Set aside for 10 minutes.

Meanwhile, in a jug (pitcher), combine the olive oil, lemon juice and vinegar and whisk until thickened and emulsified.

Drain the bread, then squeeze dry. In a food processor, combine the bread, garlic and walnuts. With the motor running, slowly pour the oil mixture into the food processor. Add the remaining ingredients and blitz to combine.

With the food processor running, slowly add up to 4 tablespoons of water to the mixture to form a smooth paste. Transfer to a serving bowl, then drizzle with olive oil and sprinkle over the parsley.

Serve with flatbreads and pickles.

AUBERGINE AND YOGURT MEZZE

Serves 4–6

2 large aubergines (eggplants) (700 g/ 1 lb 9 oz)
4 garlic cloves, minced
1 teaspoon ground cumin
½ teaspoon ground coriander
¼ teaspoon cayenne pepper
4 tablespoons tahini
4 tablespoons Greek yogurt
Juice of 1 lemon
Salt and black pepper
Extra-virgin olive oil, for drizzling
Sprig of parsley, finely chopped
1 tablespoon toasted walnuts
½ teaspoon sumac
Pitta breads or vegetable crudités, to serve

A cousin of the more commonly known *baba ghanoush*, this smoky aubergine (eggplant) dip (known as *mutabal*) is enriched with thick yogurt and nutty tahini. It's creamy, indulgent and often served more decoratively, rippled with olive oil and sprinkled with herbs and colourful spices.

Preheat the oven to 220°C/425°F/Gas Mark 7.

Place the aubergines (eggplants) in a roasting pan and roast for 30–40 minutes, until completely soft and charred. Transfer to a chopping (cutting) board to cool for 10 minutes.

When the aubergines are cool enough to handle, peel away the skins. Discard the skins and stalks. Transfer the flesh to a colander to drain, pressing down with the back of a spoon to extract as much liquid as possible.

Return the aubergines to a chopping board and finely chop. Transfer to a mixing bowl.

In a separate bowl, combine the garlic, spices, tahini, yogurt, and lemon juice. Season well with salt and pepper. Add the tahini mixture to the bowl of aubergines and mix well. Season to taste with more lemon, salt and pepper.

Transfer the mixture to a serving platter. Using a teaspoon, make indents all over the surface. Drizzle over the olive oil so that it pools in some of the indents, then sprinkle with parsley, walnuts and sumac.

Serve at room temperature with toasted pitta breads or vegetable crudités.

It can be stored in an airtight container in the refrigerator for up to 3 days.

POLENTA CRISPS WITH HERBY OLIVE SALSA

Serves 6–8

For the crisps

2½ teaspoons salt

300 g/10½ oz (generous 2 cups) instant polenta

1 tablespoon Aleppo pepper

1 tablespoon thyme leaves

Vegetable oil, for frying

100 g/3½ oz (⅔ cup) semolina (farina)

For the salsa

1 green chilli, seeded and roughly chopped

Small bunch of mint, leaves only

120 g/4 oz (1 cup) Nocellara olives, pitted

3 tablespoons pistachios, lightly toasted

1 teaspoon coriander seeds, toasted

½ teaspoon sugar

100 ml/3½ fl oz (scant ½ cup) extra-virgin olive oil

1 teaspoon white wine vinegar

I adore the wobbly consistency of soft polenta, but sometimes only something crisp and crunchy will do. These polenta crisps are best the day they're cooked and can be adapted with different herbs and spices if you have any favourites. I love the combination of woody thyme and the gentle heat from the Aleppo pepper, but Za'atar (page 254) or fresh rosemary would be lovely in their place.

Make the crisps. Bring 1 litre/34 fl oz (4¼ cups) of water to a boil, then add the salt. Pour in the polenta, whisking continuously, until smooth. Reduce the heat to medium, then cook the polenta for 15 minutes, stirring occasionally with a rubber spatula, until the polenta has a thick, porridge-like consistency. Stir in the Aleppo pepper and thyme. Turn off the heat.

Grease 4 large baking sheets with a little oil. Lay a 25 × 35-cm/ 10 × 14-inch piece of parchment paper on each. Divide the polenta between the paper, then use a rubber spatula to spread out the polenta, about 3 mm/⅛ inch thick. Set aside for 20 minutes, until set.

Meanwhile, make the salsa. Combine all the ingredients in a food processor. Pulse 10–15 times, until chunky. Season to taste with more vinegar or sugar. Transfer to a bowl and cover until ready to serve.

Heat the vegetable oil in a large saucepan to a depth of 4 cm/ 1½ inches deep over medium-high heat. The oil is ready when a cube of bread dropped in sizzles on contact and turns golden in 20 seconds. (Alternatively, use a thermometer and heat to 180°C/350°F.) Line a baking sheet with paper towels.

Place the semolina (farina) into a shallow bowl. Cut the set polenta into 3-cm/1¼-inch squares. Working in batches of 6 squares, toss the polenta in the semolina to coat. Deep-fry the polenta for 2 minutes each side, until golden and some pieces have puffed up. Using a slotted spoon, transfer the polenta crisps to the prepared baking sheet. Keep warm in a low oven. Repeat with the remaining polenta and semolina.

Transfer the crisps to a large serving bowl and serve with the salsa.

ZA'ATAR FRIES

Serves 6

1.5 kg/3 lb 5 oz floury (baking) potatoes, peeled and cut into 1-cm/½-inch batons
6 tablespoons vegetable oil, for baking
2 tablespoons Za'atar (page 254)
Salt and black pepper
Mayonnaise, to serve (optional)

I like to pre-soak the fries in cold water to remove excess starch from the potatoes. I also season the chips at the very end of cooking – if added during cooking, salt softens vegetables by drawing out moisture and causing them to steam in the oven. Be sure the oil gets nice and hot so the potatoes begin to crisp as soon as they go into the oven.

Fill a large bowl with cold water. Add the potatoes and submerge for 30 minutes.

Preheat the oven to 220°C/425°F/Gas Mark 7.

Divide the oil between 2 large roasting pans, then place them in the oven to heat up.

Meanwhile, drain the potatoes and pat dry with paper towels.

Carefully divide the potatoes between the hot pans, spreading them out into single layers. (They will steam up if they are tightly packed.) Bake for 30–40 minutes, occasionally giving the pans a good shake, until the fries are crisp and golden. Using a slotted spoon, transfer the fries to a paper towel–lined plate to drain.

In a large bowl, combine the fries, za'atar, salt and pepper. Serve immediately, with a bowl of mayonnaise alongside, if desired.

SESAME HALLOUMI FRIES WITH CHILLI YOGURT

Serves 6

For the dip

1 lime

150 g/5½ oz (scant ¾ cup) Greek yogurt

1 garlic clove, grated

½ bunch coriander (cilantro), leaves only, roughly chopped

1 teaspoon agave syrup

½ teaspoon chilli flakes

Salt and black pepper

For the halloumi fries

2 x (250-g/9-oz) packs halloumi, soaked in cold water for 1 hour

50 g/1¾ oz (⅓ cup) plain (all-purpose) flour

1 egg, beaten

70 g/2½ oz (1½ cups) panko breadcrumbs

1 tablespoon white sesame seeds

1 tablespoon black sesame seeds

Vegetable oil, for frying

These crispy, cheesy fries are deliciously addictive and perfect for a hungry crowd. (Simply double or triple the recipe as needed.) They should also be enjoyed immediately as halloumi can toughen and go rubbery as it cools.

Japanese panko breadcrumbs are made from white, crustless bread and result in a particularly crisp coating when fried. If panko breadcrumbs are tricky to find, use regular white breadcrumbs instead.

Make the dip. Zest the lime, then cut the lime into wedges. In a small bowl, combine all the ingredients, except for the lime wedges. Season to taste with salt and pepper. Set aside.

Pat dry the halloumi, then cut into 1-cm/½-inch-wide batons. Place the flour in a shallow plate and the egg into a bowl. Combine the breadcrumbs and sesame seeds on another plate. Working in small batches, coat the halloumi in the flour, then dip them in the egg. Toss them in the breadcrumb mixture until coated.

Pour enough oil into a frying pan or skillet to cover the base of the pan by 1 cm/½-inch. Heat the oil over medium-high heat. The oil is ready when a cube of bread dropped in sizzles on contact and turns golden in 20 seconds. (Alternatively, use a thermometer and heat to 180°C/350°F.) Line a baking sheet with paper towels.

Divide the halloumi into 3 batches, then carefully lower a batch into the hot oil and pan-fry for 3–4 minutes on each side, until golden and crispy. Using a slotted spoon, transfer the halloumi to the prepared baking sheet. Repeat with the remaining batches.

Serve the halloumi fries immediately with the yogurt dip and lime wedges on the side.

SMALL PLATES

L–R Parsnip and Cumin Beignets (page 44), Caramelised Onion and Tofu Pastries (page 45).

AKAWI CHEESE WITH HONEY

Serves 4 as a side

- 1 (400-g/14-oz) block akawi cheese, cut in half and sliced into 2-cm/¾-inch thick rectangles
- 2 eggs, beaten
- 1 teaspoon dried oregano or thyme
- 1 teaspoon black sesame seeds
- 80 g/¾ oz (½ cup) semolina (farina)
- Vegetable oil, for shallow frying
- 2 teaspoons runny honey
- Dill, to garnish
- Lebanese Flatbreads (page 198), to serve
- Salad, to serve

Akawi is a Middle Eastern cheese that has been soaked in brine for days to flavour and preserve it. Though different from halloumi, it still belongs in the same category of salty cheeses that can be cooked. As it does not retain its shape over heat in the same way as halloumi, take care not to overcrowd them when roasting; otherwise, you'll be left with one big melted cheese layer.

Pat dry the cheese with paper towels.

Place the eggs in a bowl. Combine the oregano or thyme and sesame seeds on a small plate and mix together. Place the semolina (farina) in a separate bowl.

Dip a piece of cheese in the egg, then roll it in the seasoning mix. Toss in the semolina (farina).

Heat the oil in a frying pan or skillet to a depth of 3 mm/⅛ inch over medium-high heat. Working in batches, add the cheese and pan-fry for 3 minutes. Turn and fry for another 3 minutes, until golden brown all over. Drain on a paper towel–lined plate, then keep warm in a low oven. Repeat with the remaining cheese.

Drizzle the honey over the cheese, then garnish with the dill. Serve the akawi warm with flatbreads and salad.

CHEESE AND HERB PASTRIES

Makes 24

200 g/7 oz goat's cheese
¼ teaspoon allspice
¼ teaspoon ground coriander
¼ teaspoon ground cumin
1 egg, beaten
½ small bunch parsley, leaves only, roughly chopped
½ small bunch dill, leaves only, roughly chopped
½ small bunch coriander (cilantro), leaves only, roughly chopped
8 sheets filo (phyllo) pastry, each cut into 3 long strips
100 g/3½ oz butter, melted

Sometimes known as *sambousek*, these stuffed deep-fried pastries are the Levant's answer to samosas. It's thought that a version of these flaky pastries travelled with the Sephardic Jews through North Africa to eventually reach Spain, where they became *empanadas*. Wherever you are in the world, there's nothing quite as satisfying as a crunchy pastry with a warm filling.

They can be filled with all manner of vegetables, lentils and cheeses. I lace mine with subtle spices and bake them for a lighter take on tradition.

Preheat the oven to 180°C/350°F/Gas Mark 4. Line a baking sheet with parchment paper.

In a bowl, combine the goat's cheese, spices and egg. Mix well, then stir in the herbs.

Brush a filo (phyllo) strip with melted butter. Place a teaspoon of the cheese mixture in one corner of the strip. Fold the corner up to meet the opposite side to form a triangle with a filo pastry 'tail' facing away from you. Continue to fold until all the filo is folded into a triangle. Brush all over with melted butter and place on the prepared baking sheet. Repeat with the remaining filling and filo.

Bake for 25 minutes, until crisp and golden. Serve warm.

SPICED TOMATO AND BEAN SAMOSAS

Makes about 30

3 tablespoons olive oil, plus extra for brushing
1 onion, thinly sliced
Salt and black pepper
2 garlic cloves, finely chopped
3 tablespoons tomato purée (paste)
1 teaspoon ground coriander
1 teaspoon cumin seeds
1 teaspoon nigella seeds, plus extra to garnish
½ teaspoon ground cinnamon
¼ teaspoon chilli flakes
1 x (400-g/14-oz) can cannellini beans, drained
Grated zest and juice of 1 lime
75 g/2¾ oz (⅔ cup) toasted walnuts, coarsely chopped
Bunch of mint, leaves only, chopped
Small bunch of spring onions (scallions), sliced diagonally
10 sheets filo (phyllo) pastry, each cut into 3 long strips
Mango Amba Sauce (page 259) or mango chutney, to serve

It's believed that samosas, a well-known Indian food staple, originated in the Middle East and travelled through Asia, following the movement of traders and invaders from the Turkic region during the Middle Ages.

Whatever their origin story, the principles are shared wherever they're cooked – a triangular pastry is filled with vegetables or meats and spices, then served piping hot from the fryer with some kind of chutney. My Mango Amba Sauce (page 259) has the perfect balance of sweet and spicy and is the ideal accompaniment.

Heat the oil in a large frying pan or skillet over medium heat. Add the onion and a pinch of salt and sauté for 6–8 minutes, until soft and golden. Add the garlic and sauté for another minute, until fragrant. Add the tomato purée (paste), spices and beans. Fry for 5 minutes, stirring occasionally, until fragrant and the beans begin to soften. Using the back of a wooden spoon, roughly mash half of the beans and leave the remaining half whole for a chunky texture. Transfer the mixture to a bowl, then add the lime zest and juice.

Stir in the walnuts, mint and spring onions (scallions). Season to taste with salt and pepper.

Preheat the oven to 220°C/425°F/Gas Mark 7. Line a baking sheet with parchment paper.

Keep the pile of filo (phyllo) covered while you prepare each samosa. Brush a strip of filo all over with oil. Place a heaped teaspoon of the mixture in one corner of the strip. Fold the corner up to meet the opposite side to start to form a triangle with a filo pastry 'tail' facing away from you. Continue to fold until all the filo is folded into a triangle. Brush with oil and sprinkle over a few nigella seeds to garnish. Place it on the prepared baking sheet. Repeat with the remaining filling and filo.

Bake for 20 minutes, until crisp and golden. Serve with the mango amba sauce or chutney.

FATAYER WITH SPINACH AND CHICKPEAS

Makes 12

For the pastry

200 g/7 oz (1¾ cups) self-raising flour, plus extra for dusting

¼ teaspoon bicarbonate of soda (baking soda)

Pinch of salt

120 ml/4 fl oz (½ cup) Greek yogurt

3 tablespoons butter, melted

1 tablespoon olive oil

For the filling

1 red Romano pepper, cut in half and seeded

450 g/1 lb spinach leaves

1–2 garlic cloves, crushed

2 spring onions (scallions), finely chopped

Pinch of cayenne pepper or paprika

150 g/5½ oz crumbled feta

100 g/3½ oz canned or cooked chickpeas, roughly chopped

Salt and black pepper

Olive oil, for brushing

Sesame seeds, for sprinkling

Photo on page 36.

Made with a very light, pillowy yogurt pastry, these pastries are best eaten straight from the oven.

I serve them as a snack or a lunch with salad, always drizzled with a thick garlic tahini sauce. Spinach is the most popular filling in my house, but I've made delicious versions with chard, kale and herbs when they're in plentiful supply.

Preheat the oven to 190°C/375°F/Gas Mark 5. Line a baking sheet with parchment paper.

Make the pastry. In a large bowl, sift together the flour, bicarbonate of soda (baking soda) and salt. Add the yogurt, melted butter and olive oil and mix until soft and pliable. Cover the dough with cling film (plastic wrap) and set aside to rest.

Make the filling. Preheat the grill (broiler) to high. Place the red pepper, cut side down, on a baking sheet and grill until the skin is charred. Transfer the roasted pepper into a bowl, cover tightly with cling film and set aside for 15 minutes.

Meanwhile, steam the spinach for 3 minutes. Drain, then squeeze out all the liquid and roughly chop. Set aside.

Take the pepper out of the bowl and remove and discard the skin. Finely dice the flesh.

In a large bowl, combine the red pepper, garlic, spring onions (scallions) and cayenne together. Add the feta, spinach and chickpeas and mix in. Season well with salt and pepper.

Divide the dough into 12 portions. Roll each into a ball. On a clean surface dusted with flour, roll out each ball into a disk, about 10 cm/4 inches in diameter. Divide the filling into 12, then place a portion in the centre of each pastry circle. Dampen the edges of the pastry with water. Bring the sides of the pastry circle together to form a half-moon. Press the seams together, then brush with oil and sprinkle with sesame seeds. Place them on the prepared baking sheet.

Bake for 20 minutes, until crisp and golden.

CHEESY SWEETCORN NUGGETS

Makes about 25

1 x (340-g/12-oz) can sweetcorn, drained
100 g/3½ oz (1 cup) grated mozzarella
100 g/3½ oz full-fat cream cheese
1 shallot, finely chopped
1 mild red chilli, finely chopped
Handful of coriander (cilantro) leaves, roughly chopped
55 g/2 oz (scant ½ cup) fine ground polenta
50 g/1¾ oz (⅓ cup) plain (all-purpose) flour
1 tablespoon cornflour (cornstarch)
½ teaspoon ground turmeric
½ teaspoon baking powder
½ teaspoon fine salt
1 egg, beaten
Black pepper
475 ml/16 fl oz (2 cups) vegetable oil, for frying
75 g/2¾ oz (1½ cups) panko breadcrumbs
4 lime wedges, to serve
Chilli Oil (page 257), to serve

Photo includes Fatayer with Spinach and Chickpeas on page 35.

There's nothing quite like the taste of corn on the cob when the sun is shining and summer is in full swing. When that time seems far away, I prepare this with canned sweetcorn, to transport me somewhere warm.

Lying somewhere between a fritter and a fried pastry, these tasty nuggets are given an extra serving of heat when drizzled with my Chilli Oil (page 257).

In a mixing bowl, combine the sweetcorn, mozzarella, cream cheese and shallot and mix well with a rubber spatula. Stir in the chilli, coriander (cilantro), polenta, flour and cornflour (cornstarch). Add the turmeric, baking powder, salt and egg and mix. Season well with pepper. Transfer to the refrigerator for 20 minutes to firm up.

Meanwhile, heat the oil in a saucepan to a depth of 3 cm/1¼ inches over medium-high heat. The oil is ready when a cube of bread dropped in sizzles on contact and turns golden in 20 seconds. (Alternatively, use a thermometer and heat to 180°C/350°F.)

Remove the sweetcorn mixture from the refrigerator. Spread the panko breadcrumbs on a large plate. Line a baking sheet with paper towels.

Using a dessertspoon, scoop heaped pieces of the sweetcorn mixture. With clean hands, roll in the panko breadcrumbs until the corn is completely covered and the size of a ping-pong ball. (This is a slightly sticky and messy job, but that's all part of the fun!) Make 5 nuggets.

Carefully lower the nuggets into the pan. Deep-fry for 2–3 minutes on each side until deep golden all over. Using a slotted spoon, transfer the nuggets to the prepared baking sheet to drain. Keep warm in a low oven. Repeat with the remaining nuggets.

Serve immediately with lime wedges and chilli oil.

CHEESY ZA'ATAR SWIRLS

Makes 10

1 x (320 g/11¼ oz) sheet puff pastry
1 tablespoon extra-virgin olive oil
2 tablespoons Za'atar (page 254)
100 g/3½ oz halloumi, grated
75 g/2¾ oz (¾ cup) grated mozzarella
2 tablespoons pine nuts
Milk, for brushing

A perfect addition to any picnic or with a drink before dinner, these pinwheel swirls couldn't be any easier to make. Children love to help fill and shape the rolls, which also make a great snack.

I often make a large batch and freeze them so I can prepare something spontaneously for unexpected guests. If freezing, place them flat on a tray until frozen, then transfer them to a sealable bag. When cooking from frozen, bake for 25–30 minutes.

Preheat the oven to 200°C/400°F/Gas Mark 6. Line a work surface with a large sheet of parchment paper. Line a baking sheet with parchment paper.

Unroll the puff pastry onto the parchment paper on the work surface, then brush the pastry with the oil. Sprinkle the za'atar, halloumi and mozzarella evenly over the pastry. Scatter over the pine nuts. Using the parchment underneath the pastry, roll it into a tight Swiss roll shape from one of the shorter edges to the other. Place on a tray and refrigerate for 15 minutes.

Using a serrated knife, cut the pastry into 2-cm/¾-inch-thick slices. Place each one, cut side up, to expose the swirl on the prepared baking sheet.

Brush each roll with a little milk. Bake for 22–25 minutes, until the pastry is flaky and golden all over. Serve warm.

Leftover swirls can be stored for up to 3 days. Gently reheat in the oven before serving.

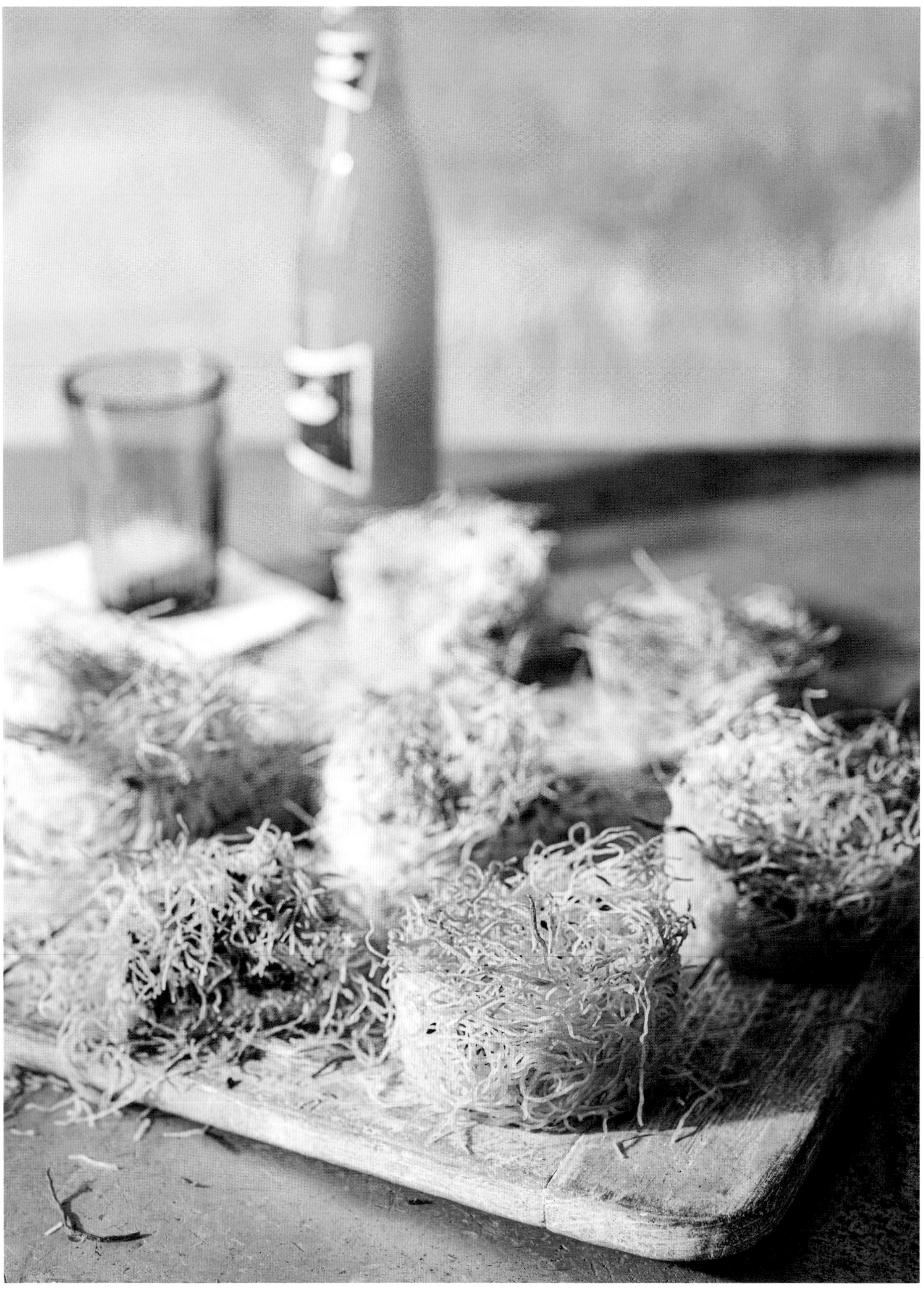

KALE AND CHEESE KATAIFI BAKES

Makes 12

300 g/10½ oz kataifi pastry, thawed if frozen

75 g/2¾ oz butter, melted, plus extra for greasing

70 g/2½ oz kale, stalks removed

125 g/4¼ oz crumbled feta

100 g/3½ oz halloumi, grated

100 g/3½ oz (scant ½ cup) ricotta

1 teaspoon dried mint

1 teaspoon sumac

1 tablespoon black sesame seeds or nigella seeds

These cute little savoury pastries are made with kataifi, a stringy filo (phyllo) pastry, commonly found in the freezer section of Middle Eastern shops.

When shaped into cups, they remind me of bird's nests. I use feta, halloumi and mild ricotta in these bakes, but they're incredibly adaptable and most cheese combinations will work well.

Preheat the oven to 180°C/350°F/Gas Mark 4.

Place the kataifi pastry in a bowl, then pour over the melted butter. With clean hands, 'pull' the butter through the strands, until all the pastry is coated.

Bring a saucepan of generously salted water to a boil. Add the kale and blanch for a minute. Drain in a colander, then set aside until cool enough to handle. With clean hands, squeeze out as much liquid from the leaves as possible. Finely chop the kale, then place in a small bowl. Stir in the feta, halloumi, ricotta, mint and sumac.

Grease a 12-cup muffin pan, then divide roughly half of the pastry between the holes. Use the bottom of an espresso cup or small glass to pack down the pastry, using a push and twist motion. Repeat 5–6 times over each hole, so the pastry strands stick together. Divide the cheese mixture between the holes, leaving a 5-mm/¼-inch border around the edges. Dot the remaining pastry over the cheese mixture, tucking in the cheese as you go. Use the same espresso cup or glass to press down on the top 3–4 times. Sprinkle the seeds on top of each.

Bake for 18–20 minutes, until the pastry is deep golden and crisp. Set aside to cool in the pan, then use a palette knife to release them. Serve warm.

Cooled kataifi bakes can be stored in an airtight container for 3 days. When ready to serve, warm them in an oven preheated to 160°C/325°F/Gas Mark 3 for 5 minutes.

HALLOUMI AND ZA'ATAR SPRING ROLLS

Makes 16

- 1 x (225-g/8-oz) block halloumi, soaked in cold water for 1 hour
- 16 square wonton or spring roll wrappers
- Small bunch of mint, leaves only, roughly chopped
- Light olive oil, for frying
- Grated zest and juice of 1 lemon
- 2 tablespoons Za'atar (page 254), for sprinkling
- Chilli Oil (page 257), to serve

Crispy, hot and cheesy, these spring rolls embody all that is good about Levantine street food. Soaking the halloumi before cooking draws out some of its preserving salt, and thus helps to soften the cheese. Try this tip and rubbery, overly salty halloumi will be a thing of the past.

Drain the halloumi, then pat dry with paper towels. Cut into 16 batons, about 1 cm/½ inch thick.

Fill a small bowl with cold water. Arrange the wonton wrappers on a work surface. Working one at a time, place a piece of halloumi in the centre of a wonton wrapper. Sprinkle with a little mint. Dip a finger in the water bowl, then run your finger along the wrapper edge to moisten. Fold up the wrapper, tucking in the sides. Press the edges together with wet fingers to seal. Repeat with the remaining wrappers, halloumi and mint.

Heat the oil in a large frying pan or skillet to a depth of 2 mm/1⁄16 inch over medium heat, until it shimmers. Carefully lower a spring roll into the oil. If it sizzles immediately, the oil is hot enough. Fry the spring rolls for 2–3 minutes on each side, until crisp and golden. Using tongs, transfer the spring rolls to a paper towel–lined plate to drain. Sprinkle immediately with lemon zest, juice and za'atar. Repeat with the remaining spring rolls.

Serve immediately with the chilli oil for dipping.

NF

PARSNIP AND CUMIN BEIGNETS

Makes about 30

For the beignets

750 g/1 lb 10 oz parsnips, peeled and cut into 3-cm/1¼-inch chunks

1 litre/34 fl oz (4¼ cups) milk

2 fresh bay leaves

3 black peppercorns

200 g/7 oz (1¼ cups) plain (all-purpose) flour

1 teaspoon baking powder

75 g/2¾ oz halloumi, grated

1 tablespoon cumin seeds, toasted

100 g/3½ oz (1½ cups) fine breadcrumbs

Vegetable oil, for deep frying

Flaky sea salt, for sprinkling

For the garlic yogurt

250 g/9 oz (1 cup plus 2 tablespoons) Greek yogurt

2 sprigs mint, leaves only, finely chopped

1 garlic clove, grated

½ teaspoon salt

Photo on page 28.

Root vegetables are a staple in the UK. They were prevalent when I moved here in the 1960s, offering a cheap, filling and nourishing option for families who hadn't yet embraced convenience food culture. I initially found them a bit bland compared to the spiced and richly flavoured food of Lebanon. But with a little help from careful cooking and accompanying flavours to balance out their sweet, earthy character, parsnips have become one of my favourite vegetables. This recipe would also work well with potatoes.

Make the beignets. In a large saucepan, combine the parsnips, milk, bay leaves and peppercorns. Cover and bring to a boil. Reduce the heat to medium-low and gently simmer for 25 minutes, until the parsnips are completely soft.

Using a slotted spoon, transfer the parsnips to the bowl of a food processor. Process until completely smooth. You should be left with about 600 g/1 lb 5 oz parsnip purée.

Sift the flour and baking powder into a large mixing bowl. Using a rubber spatula, fold in the parsnips until incorporated into the mixture. Add the halloumi and cumin seeds and fold again to combine. Cover the bowl, then allow the dough to rest for 1 hour.

Meanwhile, make the garlic yogurt. Combine all the ingredients in a bowl and mix well. Cover and refrigerate until ready to serve.

Spread the breadcrumbs on a tray. Using a teaspoon, scoop heaped pieces from the dough. Toss to coat.

Heat the oil in a saucepan to a depth of 7.5 cm/3 inches over medium-high heat. The oil is ready when a cube of bread dropped in sizzles on contact and turns golden in 20 seconds. (Alternatively, use a thermometer and heat to 180°C/350°F.) Working in batches to avoid overcrowding, carefully lower the coated dough into the hot oil and deep-fry for 2–3 minutes until golden and crisp. Using a slotted spoon, transfer the beignets onto a paper towel–lined plate. Keep warm in a low oven with the door slightly ajar. Repeat with the remaining dough.

Arrange the beignets on a platter alongside a bowl of the yogurt. Sprinkle with the flaky sea salt and serve immediately.

NF

SPICED CARAMELISED ONION AND TOFU PASTRIES

Makes 12

2 tablespoons ghee
1 tablespoon light olive oil
3 onions, thinly sliced
Salt and black pepper
2 garlic cloves, crushed
2 teaspoons ground cumin
1 teaspoon ground coriander
½ teaspoon ground turmeric
¼ teaspoon ground ginger
⅛ teaspoon cayenne pepper
⅛ teaspoon ground allspice
2 tomatoes, roughly chopped
3 tablespoons tomato purée (paste)
450 g/1 lb firm tofu, squeezed over a colander to remove as much water as possible, grated
Juice of ½ lemon
Small bunch of coriander (cilantro), leaves only, chopped
2 x sheets 320 g/11¼ oz ready-rolled shortcrust pastry (basic pie dough)
1 egg, beaten
1 teaspoon nigella seeds

Photo on page 29.

Piping hot Cornish pasties, filled with gently spiced vegetables and meats, are a cornerstone of British culinary tradition. While I'm partial to a pasty, I'm also a big fan of spice and vibrant herbs, so this is my Levantine interpretation. After all, food culture is constantly evolving, and new recipes are inspired by old ones.

Rather untraditionally, I use ready-rolled shortcrust pastry (basic pie dough) to save time. Just be sure to completely cool the filling before shaping the pastries, otherwise the dough will melt and tear.

Preheat the oven to 200°C/400°F/Gas Mark 6.

Heat the ghee and oil in a large frying pan or skillet over medium-high heat, until it shimmers. Add the onions and a generous pinch of salt and sauté for 8 minutes, until the onions are soft. Reduce the heat to low, then sauté for another 15 minutes, until the onions are caramelised and have reduced in volume by a third.

Increase the heat to medium, then add a splash of water to the pan. Using a wooden spoon, loosen up any bits of onion clinging to the base. Add the garlic and spices and cook for a minute, until deeply fragrant. Stir in the tomatoes, tomato purée (paste) and a pinch of salt and sauté for 6–8 minutes, until the tomatoes have broken down and the mixture looks saucy.

Stir in the grated tofu. Sauté for 10 minutes, until the liquid has evaporated from the pan and the tofu is stained bright yellow from the turmeric. Remove from the heat.

Stir in the lemon juice and coriander (cilantro). Season to taste with more salt and pepper. Cool to room temperature before filling the pastry. (Otherwise, the fat in the pastry will melt, creating holes in the pastries and causing the filling to escape as it cooks.)

Line 2 large baking sheets with parchment paper. Unroll the pastry, then cut each into 6 squares. Place 2 tablespoons of the filling in each square. Bring one corner up over the filling to meet the opposite corner and press down on the edges with the tines of a fork to seal. Place on the prepared baking sheet. Repeat with the remaining squares and filling.

Brush the pastries with the beaten egg, then sprinkle over the nigella seeds. Bake for 28–30 minutes, until deep golden and crispy. Serve warm or at room temperature.

CHICKPEA PANCAKES

Serves 8

150 g/5½ oz (1½ cups) gram flour
1 teaspoon salt
¼ teaspoon cayenne pepper
4 tablespoons extra-virgin olive oil
2 tablespoons Za'atar (page 254)
Dill, for sprinkling

If I had a restaurant of my own, I'd serve za'atar shakers on the table, alongside the salt and pepper. This simple savoury pancake can be eaten hot on its own as a snack or presented as a base for the Spiced Lentil and Pine Nut Curry (page 128). Whatever you do, don't scrimp on the za'atar.

I make my own jars of za'atar to have on-hand and to give out to friends and family, but there are some great versions available now from larger supermarkets. Look for a fine powder with flecks of whole sesame seeds throughout the mix.

In a large bowl, combine the gram flour, salt and cayenne pepper. Gradually whisk in 250 ml/8 fl oz (1 cup) warm water, until the mixture is smooth. Cover and set aside to ferment for at least 1 hour or up to 24 hours for a more complex flavour.

When ready to eat, preheat the oven to 220°C/425°F/Gas Mark 7. Whisk 1 tablespoon of the olive oil into the batter.

Heat 2 tablespoons of the oil in a large oven-proof frying pan or skillet over medium heat for 2 minutes, until the oil is sizzling. Pour in the chickpea batter and cook for 5 minutes, until the sides are set and beginning to look crisp and golden on the outside.

Sprinkle over the za'atar, then place the pan in the oven and bake for 10 minutes. Drizzle over the remaining tablespoon of oil and sprinkle with the dill. Serve whole or cut into wedges.

Alternatively, heat a little of the oil in a frying pan and cook a ladleful of the batter at a time for thinner, individual pancakes.

Photo includes Spiced Lentil and Pine Nut Curry on page 128.

RICOTTA BALLS WITH PRESERVED LEMON AND ALEPPO PEPPER

Serves 4–6

For the ricotta balls

500 g/1 lb 2 oz (scant 1 cup) ricotta, drained

50 g/1¾ oz hard goat's or sheep cheese, finely grated

½ teaspoon grated nutmeg

½ teaspoon salt

Black pepper

300 g/10½ oz (2 cups) fine semolina (farina)

Extra-hard goat's cheese, crumbled (optional)

For the quick preserved lemon

Pared zest and juice of 2 lemons

½ teaspoon fine salt

½ teaspoon sugar

For the Aleppo pepper sauce

100 g/3½ oz butter

3 sprigs thyme, leaves only

1 teaspoon Aleppo pepper

If I could choose my last meal on earth, this would be one of the (many) courses. These cloud-like ricotta balls are my reimagination of Italian *gnudi*, cheese dumplings coated in semolina (farina), which form a skin to protect the fresh cheese inside when cooked in salted water. Here, I've given them a Middle Eastern twist with the addition of quick preserved lemon (an essential in your culinary arsenal) and Aleppo pepper.

The ricotta balls need to be refrigerated for three days before cooking, so some advanced planning may be required.

Make the ricotta balls. Line a plate with paper towels, then spread out the ricotta thinly with a rubber spatula. Cover with paper towels and refrigerate for 20 minutes.

In a mixing bowl, combine the ricotta, cheese and nutmeg. Season with the salt and pepper to taste.

Place half of the semolina (farina) onto a baking sheet. Shape the ricotta mixture into 5-cm/2-inch balls and add to the baking sheet. Pour over the remaining semolina to coat. Transfer the tray to the refrigerator and turn the balls once a day for 3 days. The semolina eventually forms a coating around the ricotta balls, like a thin pasta.

On the third day, make the quick preserved lemon. Combine all the ingredients in a saucepan. Add 2 tablespoons of water. Bring to a boil over medium heat and boil until the liquid has thickened to a thick gel-like consistency and the lemon zest has puckered. Remove the lemons from the pan, finely chop them and set aside.

For the sauce, melt half of the butter in a frying pan or skillet over medium heat, until it bubbles. Add the thyme and Aleppo pepper and fry until the butter darkens and begins to smell nutty. Remove from the heat.

Preheat the oven to 150°C/300°F/Gas Mark 3.

Bring a saucepan of water to a boil. Working in batches to avoid overcrowding, gently lower the ricotta balls into the pan. Cook for 3–4 minutes, until the balls bob to the surface of the water. Keep the cooked ricotta balls warm in an ovenproof bowl in the oven. Repeat with the remaining ricotta balls.

Transfer 3 tablespoons of the starchy cooking water to another frying pan or skillet. Add the remaining butter and heat over medium heat, shaking occasionally, until the sauce emulsifies and thickens.

Serve the ricotta balls on warm plates and drizzle both butter sauces evenly between each plate. Sprinkle with preserved lemon and serve immediately.

BLACK LIME AND HERB TOFU

Serves 2

250 g/9 oz firm tofu, patted dry and crumbled into roughly 2-cm/¾-inch pieces

150 g/5½ oz (1 cup) rice flour

400 ml/14 fl oz (1⅔ cups) groundnut (peanut) or vegetable oil

3 black limes, crushed into pieces with your hands

3 tablespoons Fermented Red Onions (page 64)

4 tablespoons extra-virgin olive oil

2 red onions, finely chopped

½ teaspoon salt

4 garlic cloves, finely chopped

2 tablespoons tomato purée (paste)

1 teaspoon ground coriander

¼ teaspoon ground cumin

100 g/3½ oz coriander (cilantro)

100 g/3½ oz parsley, stems finely chopped and leaves roughly chopped

100 g/3½ oz dill, stems finely chopped and leaves roughly chopped

Lebanese Flatbreads (page 198) or Lime and Herb Baked Rice (page 139), to serve

In the Levant, herbs are treated as another vegetable, so don't shy away from the amount used in this recipe – the herbs wilt down to make a deeply aromatic sauce to coat the tofu. I buy herbs from the local greengrocer or Middle Eastern shops, which come in bigger (and cheaper) bunches. If you struggle to get hold of 300 g/10½ oz of herbs, you can substitute the balance of the weight with spinach.

This recipe calls for the Fermented Red Onions (page 64) but you can also use the quick pickle recipe on page 90 and marinate for 30 minutes. The flavour won't be the same, but it will be a decent stand-in.

In a large bowl, combine the tofu and rice flour and toss to coat.

Heat the groundnut (peanut) oil in a medium saucepan over medium-high heat to a temperature of 170°C/340°F. Working in batches, add the tofu and pan-fry for 2–3 minutes. Using a slotted spoon, gingerly turn the pieces over and pan-fry for another 2–3 minutes, until crisp and golden. Using the same slotted spoon, transfer the tofu to a paper towel-lined plate to drain. Repeat with the remaining tofu. Set aside.

Place the black limes in a spice grinder and grind until a fine powder forms. In a small bowl, combine the fermented red onions and a teaspoon of the black lime and mix well. Set aside.

Heat the olive oil in a large frying pan or skillet over medium heat. Add the red onions and salt and sauté for 8 minutes, until completely soft. Add the garlic, tomato purée (paste), ground coriander and cumin and the remaining dried lime. Cook for another minute, until completely fragrant. Stir in the herbs, then cover with a lid. Reduce the heat to low and sauté for 25 minutes, until the herbs are completely soft. Add the fried tofu and cook until warmed through.

Transfer to a serving plate and serve with the fermented red onions, flatbreads or lime and herb baked rice.

MINT AND PRESERVED LIME LABNEH

Serves 4

500 g/1 lb 2 oz (2¼ cups) Greek yogurt

3 tablespoons extra-virgin olive oil, plus extra for drizzling

1 Spiced Preserved Lime (page 260) or ½ preserved lemon

1 mild green chilli, finely chopped

1 teaspoon dried mint

2 handfuls of rocket (arugula) or watercress

Pomegranate Molasses (page 256), for drizzling

Lebanese Flatbreads (page 198), to serve

Labneh is a staple across the Middle East, as a cooling dip or a cheese, when rolled into balls and soaked in oil. We even mix it with honey and set it as a cheesecake for a sweet treat.

I use Greek yogurt, but it can also be made with sheep or goat's yogurt for a bold flavour.

Line a colander with a piece of muslin (cheesecloth) and suspend the colander over a bowl. Add the yogurt to the colander. Gather up the muslin sides to seal, then leave the yogurt to drain at room temperature for at least 3 hours or up to 12 for a firmer labneh. (The watery whey in the bowl can be used to make bread or replace filtered water when preserving vegetables.) Transfer the labneh to a mixing bowl.

Pour the oil into a small mixing bowl. Using a serrated knife, cut away the flesh from the preserved lime and discard. (It is too salty to eat.) Finely chop the skin, then add it to the bowl, along with the chilli and mint. Mix well. Stir the mixture into the labneh.

Spread the labneh on a platter, then top with the rocket (arugula) and drizzle with the oil and pomegranate molasses. Serve with flatbreads.

SALADS

L–R Fermented Red Onions (page 64), Fermented Beetroot and Turnips (page 65).

COURGETTE AND PITTA SALAD

Serves 2, or 4 as a starter or side

- 2 courgettes (zucchini), chopped into 4-cm/1½-inch pieces
- 1 red onion, thinly sliced
- 1 teaspoon coriander seeds
- 1 teaspoon Aleppo pepper
- 2 tablespoons extra-virgin olive oil
- 1 teaspoon salt
- 225 g/8 oz cherry tomatoes, halved
- 1 tablespoon sumac
- 2 wholemeal pitta breads, torn into bite-size pieces
- 100 g/3½ oz (generous ½ cup) pomegranate seeds
- 50 g/1¾ oz hard sheep or goat's cheese
- 2–3 sprigs dill, leaves only

I love how Italian panzanella salad combines torn pieces of stale bread with ripe tomatoes, herbs and oil. Whenever I cook a batch of pittas, there are inevitably one or two that don't get eaten immediately. By applying the principles of panzanella and adding gentle spices, roasted courgettes (zucchini) and juicy tomatoes, we've revived the pittas in a hearty and healthy, no-waste salad.

If you want to make this salad vegan, use a vegan feta-style cheese instead and add a handful of toasted nuts.

Preheat the oven to 220°C/425°F/Gas Mark 7.

In a large roasting pan, combine the courgettes (zucchini), red onion, coriander seeds, Aleppo pepper and olive oil and toss until everything is combined. Sprinkle over ½ teaspoon of salt and toss again. Roast for 30 minutes, turning the vegetables a couple of times.

Meanwhile, in another bowl, combine the tomatoes, sumac and the remaining salt. Set aside.

Remove the courgettes from the oven. Add the pitta and stir well. Roast for another 5 minutes, until the pitta is crisp.

To the bowl of tomatoes, add the roasted vegetables, pitta and pomegranate and mix well.

Transfer to a serving platter and shave over the cheese. Scatter over the dill and serve warm or cool.

FRESH AND CRUNCHY FATTOUSH

Serves 4

- 1 red onion, thinly sliced
- 2 tablespoons apple cider vinegar
- 1 teaspoon sugar
- ½ teaspoon coriander seeds
- 400 g/14 oz mixed tomatoes, chopped
- 1 teaspoon salt
- Black pepper
- 3 tablespoons extra-virgin olive oil
- 2 wholemeal pitta breads, torn into bite-size pieces
- 1 heaped tablespoon sumac
- 1 cucumber, halved lengthwise and watery seeds removed
- 1 head cos (romaine) lettuce, leaves roughly torn
- 1 heaped tablespoon Za'atar (page 254)

There's no escaping it, *fattoush* is served with nearly every meal in my homeland. It will often contain some combination of bread, cucumber, tomatoes and, crucially, sumac.

Sumac is a sharp, burgundy-coloured spice often used in place of lemon or lime. When buying it, choose small quantities or a dark spice as the intensity of flavour lessens over time as the spice is exposed to the air.

In a large bowl, combine the onion, vinegar, sugar and coriander seeds. With clean hands, scrunch until the onion begins to soften. Top with a clean jar or bowl to press down on the salad and set aside.

In a small bowl, combine the tomatoes, salt and pepper to taste. Set aside.

Heat the oil in a large frying pan or skillet over medium heat. Add the pitta and pan-fry for 8 minutes, until crispy and golden. Stir in the sumac and remove from the heat.

Chop the cucumber into 1-cm/½-inch half-moons. Add to the bowl of tomatoes and toss well. Add the lettuce and za'atar and stir again.

On a serving platter, combine the tomato mixture, pickled onions and pitta and mix well. Serve immediately.

FERMENTED RED CABBAGE

Makes 1 x (2-litre/2-quart) jar

- 1 kg/2 lb 4 oz red cabbage, outer leaves removed, cut into quarters and cored
- 1 tablespoon salt, plus extra if needed
- 1 garlic clove, thinly sliced
- 1 teaspoon sumac
- 2 fresh bay leaves

Pickled red cabbage is available at almost every falafel stand or served with shawarma to cut through the oiliness of fried foods. Here, sumac mimics the tangy flavour that comes from vinegar, but I bet fennel seeds or caraway would work well, too.

These days, I prefer healthier lacto-fermented red cabbage – it's great for gut health, plus it lasts longer! As lacto-fermentation relies on a very clean environment to work successfully, ensure your jar is sterilised, your hands well-scrubbed and your utensils are sparkling clean. When it comes to this recipe, seek out a cabbage head that feels heavy for its size, with no marks or discolouration on the leaves. You're preserving the cabbage, so it needs to be as fresh as possible to ensure no bacteria is introduced into the mixture.

Using a mandoline, thinly slice the cabbage into a large bowl. Add the salt. With clean hands, rub the salt into the cabbage for 5 minutes, until the cabbage has softened and liquid appears at the bottom of the bowl. Cover, then set aside for 1 hour.

Place the garlic, sumac and bay at the bottom of a sterilised 2-litre/2-quart Mason jar. Add a handful of cabbage into the jar and press down with your fist to pack it down tightly. Repeat until it's full. (You should start to see brine rising above the surface of the cabbage after a few handfuls.) Ensure the cabbage is completely submerged in the brine, using a rubber spatula to scrape the sides of the jar. If the brine doesn't quite cover the cabbage, mix 200 ml/7 fl oz (¾ cup plus 1 tablespoon) boiling water with 1 teaspoon of salt and stir until the salt is dissolved. Pour the brine over the cabbage, leaving a 4-cm/1½-inch headspace. Weigh the cabbage down with a clean zip-top bag, part-filled with water. Close the lid and set aside on a plate (as the brine will bubble through the gap in the lid). Store in a dark place for 7–14 days, opening every day to release the gas.

After 7 days, taste the cabbage. It should be sour and crunchy. It can be left for up to 14 days for a stronger flavour. Once you're happy with the flavour, remove the weight and store the jar in the refrigerator for up to 6 months.

FERMENTED RED ONIONS

Makes 1 x (2-litre/2-quart) jar

- 4 teaspoons fine salt
- 6 black peppercorns
- 1 cinnamon stick
- 4 red onions, thinly sliced into rings
- 1 dessert apple, cored and thinly sliced into rounds

It would be unthinkable to serve a mezze without some pickled vegetable element. While I love pickles as much as the next person, recently I've been making more fermented vegetables which give the same tang with the added benefit of good bacteria for the gut.

I like the sweetness of the apple, but you can leave it out if you prefer a sharper pickle.

Bring 1 litre/34 fl oz (4¼ cups) of water to a boil. Add the salt and stir until dissolved.

Place the spices in a sterilised 2-litre/2-quart Mason jar. Layer the onions and apple slices into the jar.

Pour the water over the onions. If the onions and apples sit above the surface of the brine, weigh them down with a clean zip-top bag partially filled with water.

Close the lid and set aside on a plate in a cool, dark place for 14 days. Open the jar every day to release the gas, before closing and resealing. If the onions and apples rise above the surface of the water, make a little more brine by mixing 200 ml/7 fl oz (¾ cup plus 1 tablespoon) boiling water with 1 teaspoon of salt and stirring until the salt is dissolved, then use as much as needed to cover, while leaving a good headspace.

After 14 days, remove the weight and discard. The onions can be stored in the refrigerator for up to 6 months.

Photo on page 56.

FERMENTED BEETROOT AND TURNIPS

Makes 1 x (2-litre/2-quart) jar

1 tablespoon salt

2 garlic cloves, thinly sliced

1 thumb-sized piece of fresh ginger, peeled and diced

Sprig of rosemary

2 beetroot (beets) (about 500 g/1 lb 2 oz), peeled and cut into matchsticks with a mandoline

1 turnip (about 250 g/9 oz), peeled and cut into matchsticks with a mandoline

These refreshing pickled root vegetables make an excellent lunch with crusty bread and creamy, soft cheese. When choosing beetroot (beets) for this recipe, look for those which have a smooth skin and feel heavy for their size.

The fermented beetroot and turnips can be stored in the refrigerator or gifted to friends – the colour is incredible.

Bring 750 ml/25 fl oz (3 cups) of water to a boil. Add the salt and stir until dissolved. Set aside to cool.

Place the garlic, ginger and rosemary in a 2-litre/2-quart Mason jar. Cover with the beetroots and turnips. Pour the brine over the beetroots and turnips, then weigh them down with a clean zip-top bag partially filled with water. The vegetables must be submerged in the brine.

Close the lid and set aside on a plate (as the brine will bubble through the gap in the lid). Store in a cool, dark place for 7 days, opening every day to release the gas. If the beetroots and turnips rise above the surface of the water, make a little more brine by mixing 200 ml/7 fl oz (¾ cup plus 1 tablespoon) boiling water with 1 teaspoon of salt and stirring until the salt is dissolved, then use as much as needed to cover, while leaving a good headspace.

After 7 days, remove the weight and discard. The pickle can be stored in the refrigerator for up to 6 months. Alternatively, divide it among smaller jars and share with family and friends.

Photo on page 57.

SUMAC AND BARBERRY HERB SALAD

Serves 4

3 tablespoons apple juice

2 tablespoons Pomegranate Molasses (page 256)

1 teaspoon maple syrup

2 teaspoons apple cider vinegar

50 g/1¾ oz (scant ½ cup) dried barberries

6 tablespoons olive oil

Salt and black pepper

Small bunch of dill, leaves picked

Small bunch of parsley, leaves picked

Small bunch of mint, leaves picked

150 g/5½ oz lettuce or mixed salad leaves (greens), washed and roughly torn

75 g/2¾ oz crumbled feta

1 tablespoon sumac

A light salad for hot days, this zesty mix is full of fresh flavours. It would be delicious with a shawarma or olive oil-laced dip alongside flatbreads.

Commonly used in Iranian cookery, barberries can be found in Middle Eastern shops and larger supermarkets, or use other tart dried fruit, such as cranberries or sour cherries, for a twist on this recipe.

In a bowl, combine the apple juice, pomegranate molasses, maple syrup and apple cider vinegar and mix well. Add the barberries and mix. Set aside for 30 minutes, until the barberries are plumped up and juicy.

Whisk in the olive oil. Season to taste with salt and pepper.

In a large mixing bowl, combine half of the barberry dressing, the herbs and salad leaves. Toss to mix. Pour the rest of the dressing into a jug (pitcher) and set aside for later.

Arrange the salad on a platter and top with the crumbled feta. Sprinkle over the sumac and drizzle with more of the barberry dressing, according to taste.

Photo includes Tomato and Pomegranate Salad on page 74.

SMOKY SUMAC ONION SALAD

Serves 4

Extra-virgin olive oil, for charring and dressing

½ teaspoon salt

4 small red onions, cut in half lengthwise with the root intact

2 tablespoons Pomegranate Molasses (page 256)

¼ teaspoon ground cardamom

100 g/3½ oz (scant ½ cup) ricotta, drained

2–3 sprigs mint, leaves thinly sliced

1 teaspoon sumac

Salt and black pepper

100 g/3½ oz (½ cup) cooked brown lentils, patted dry with paper towels

Onions are all too often the bridesmaid, forming the structure of the recipe from the outset rather than starring in the leading role. This recipe spotlights the humble onion, teasing out the jammy flavours and balancing them out with milky ricotta and tart pomegranate molasses.

Preheat the oven to 200°C/400°F/Gas Mark 6.

Heat enough oil to coat the bottom of a large frying pan or skillet over medium heat. Add the salt, then arrange the onions, cut side down in the pan. Cover and cook for 8 minutes. Increase the heat to high and cook for another 2 minutes. Using a rubber spatula, press down firmly on the onions and cook for another minute.

Transfer the onions to a baking sheet, cut side up. Brush the charred side with pomegranate molasses, sprinkle with cardamom and bake for 20 minutes. Set aside the onions.

When cool enough to handle, break the onions into layers and arrange on a large platter. Drizzle over any remaining juices from the pan. Dot the ricotta over the onions, then sprinkle with mint. In a small bowl, combine 1 tablespoon of the olive oil, sumac and a pinch of salt.

Heat 1 tablespoon of the olive oil in a frying pan or skillet over medium-high heat. Add the lentils and sauté for 5 minutes until hot and crispy. Season with salt and pepper and sprinkle over the onion salad along with the sumac oil.

WATERMELON AND FETA SALAD

Serves 6 as a side

1 red onion, thinly sliced
Juice of 1 lime
1 tablespoon apple cider vinegar
½ teaspoon sugar
1 small round watermelon, flesh chopped into 3-cm/1¼-inch pieces
1 red chilli, seeded and finely chopped
125 g/4¼ oz (1 cup) black olives, pitted and roughly chopped
Small bunch of mint, leaves only, finely chopped
100 g/3½ oz crumbled feta
Extra-virgin olive oil, for drizzling
Black pepper

I first made this salad on a rainy, grey January day when I was craving sunshine and the feeling of warmth on my cheeks. Even though it felt a long way off, the flavours on my plate transported me to where the sun really was shining.

In a large bowl, combine the red onion, lime juice, the vinegar and sugar. With clean hands, rub the liquid into the onion until it begins to soften. Place a clean jar or similar weight on top to press the onions down. Set aside for 30 minutes.

Drain the onions. Combine the onions, watermelon, chilli, olives and mint in a bowl and toss to combine.

Transfer everything to a large serving platter, then sprinkle over the feta. Generously drizzle olive oil on top and season with pepper. Serve immediately.

   30

LEBANESE CABBAGE SALAD

Serves 4

½ white cabbage (about 400 g/14 oz), thinly shaven with a mandoline
8 cherry tomatoes, diced
Small bunch of parsley, leaves only, finely chopped
1 garlic clove, minced
1 teaspoon sumac
⅛ teaspoon cayenne pepper
2 tablespoons extra-virgin olive oil
Juice of 1 lemon
Salt and black pepper

A fresh, edible jumble of the colours of the Lebanese flag (white, red and green), this refreshing cabbage salad comes together in 10 minutes. It's the perfect accompaniment to Falafel (page 146) or grilled kebabs smothered in Garlic Tahini Sauce (page 258). It can also be served as part of a mezze spread.

If using a mandoline to cut the cabbage, be sure to use the grip against the blade to protect your fingertips.

In a large bowl, combine the cabbage, tomatoes and parsley and mix to combine.

In a small bowl, combine the remaining ingredients. Pour over the cabbage mixture and toss to combine. Season to taste with salt and pepper. Set aside for 15 minutes until the flavours have mingled, then serve.

ZA'ATAR CUCUMBER NOODLE SALAD

Serves 4 as a side or 2 as a main

For the salad

1 cucumber, sliced in half crosswise

1 tablespoon apple cider vinegar

2 teaspoons sugar

½ teaspoon salt

200 g/7 oz buckwheat (soba) noodles

1 tablespoon Za'atar (page 254), plus extra to garnish

Small bunch of mint, leaves only, finely chopped, plus extra leaves to garnish

1 Spiced Preserved Lime (page 260) or ½ preserved lemon, peel only, finely chopped

4 tablespoons flaked (slivered) almonds or pistachios, toasted

For the tahini dressing

5 tablespoons tahini

1 garlic clove, minced

1½ tablespoons white miso paste

2 teaspoons apple cider vinegar, plus extra if needed

1–2 teaspoons honey, plus extra if needed

Salt and black pepper

Photo includes Shepherd's Salad on page 75.

With a combination of pickled and ribboned cucumbers, this refreshing and satisfying salad is layered with flavour.

Admittedly, the use of buckwheat (soba) noodles and miso are unconventional in Middle Eastern food. I'd categorise this as a fusion salad, taking inspiration from both Lebanon and Japan.

Make the salad. Slice one of the cucumber halves in half lengthwise. Lay the cucumber pieces, flat side down, on a chopping (cutting) board and slice diagonally into 1-cm/½-inch pieces. (This will expose more of the cucumber's surface area and help it to stay crunchy.) In a bowl, combine the sliced cucumber, vinegar, sugar and salt. Set aside.

Cook the buckwheat (soba) noodles according to the package directions. Rinse well under cold running water and shake dry.

Over a separate mixing bowl, peel the other cucumber half into ribbons, stopping when you reach the watery seeds in the middle. Discard the centre. Add the noodles, za'atar, mint and preserved lime to the bowl of cucumber ribbons. Mix well.

Make the tahini dressing. Combine all the ingredients in a jug (pitcher) and whisk. Slowly pour in up to 4 tablespoons of water, whisking between each addition until the mixture has the consistency of thick double (heavy) cream. Season to taste with more honey, vinegar, salt and/or pepper. Pour the dressing over the noodle mixture and toss to combine.

Transfer the dressed noodles to a platter. Drain the sliced cucumber and arrange over the top. Scatter over a little extra za'atar, the toasted nuts and mint leaves. Serve immediately.

The noodles can be prepared and dressed up to a day in advance, just leave out both cucumber elements until ready to serve.

TOMATO AND POMEGRANATE SALAD

Serves 4

- ½ red onion, thinly sliced into half-moons
- 1 teaspoon sugar
- 1 tablespoon white wine vinegar
- Juice from ½ lemon
- 4 ripe tomatoes, diced
- Seeds from 1 pomegranate
- Small bunch of parsley, leaves picked, finely chopped
- 1 teaspoon sumac
- 1 teaspoon dried mint
- ½ teaspoon salt
- Falafel (page 146), to serve (optional)

Photo on page 67.

Pomegranate and tomato may not feel like a natural flavour pairing, but in the Middle East, they're often served together in this salsa-like combination of juicy, fresh flavours. It can be served with grilled vegetables, halloumi and wraps, as a refreshing palate cleanser between bites. I sometimes add red chilli or change the herbs, depending on what I have in the refrigerator.

In a bowl, combine the red onion, sugar, vinegar and lemon juice. With clean hands, scrunch the mixture to separate the pieces of red onion and work in the sugar and vinegar. Set aside for 30 minutes.

In a serving bowl, combine the tomatoes, pomegranate seeds, parsley, sumac, dried mint and salt. Set aside for 30 minutes–1½ hours, until the flavours have mingled.

Drain the red onion, then stir into the salad.

Serve the salad on its own or with falafel, if desired.

SPICED CARROT SALAD

Serves 4

- 3 large carrots, grated
- ½ teaspoon ground cumin
- ¼ teaspoon ground cinnamon
- Grated zest and juice of 1 orange
- Salt and black pepper
- Small bunch of parsley, leaves only, finely chopped
- 75 g/2¾ oz (½ cup plus 2 tablespoons) toasted almonds, roughly chopped
- 40 g/1½ oz sultanas or golden raisins, soaked in warm water for 15 minutes

Photo on page 156.

I have my grandchildren help me make this fresh and easy salad as it's impossible to get wrong and incredibly adaptable with different spices, nuts, dried fruit and herbs. I like to serve it alongside cooked falafel and hummus for a colourful spread.

In a large bowl, combine the carrots, cumin, cinnamon and orange zest and juice and mix well. Season with salt and pepper. Cover, then set aside for 1 hour until the flavours have mingled. Season to taste with more salt and pepper.

Reserve a tablespoon of the parsley and almonds. Add the remaining herbs and nuts to the bowl and stir. Drain the sultanas, then stir them into the mixture.

Transfer the salad to a serving platter, then top with the reserved almonds and parsley. Serve immediately.

The salad can be stored in the refrigerator for up to 3 days.

SHEPHERD'S SALAD

Serves 4 as a side

3 juicy tomatoes, cut into 1-cm/½-inch pieces
½ teaspoon fine salt
½ cucumber, cut into 1-cm/½-inch pieces
½ bunch spring onions (scallions), thinly sliced diagonally
Small bunch of dill, leaves picked and roughly chopped
Small bunch of parsley, leaves picked and roughly chopped
Small bunch of mint, leaves picked and roughly chopped
10 black olives, pitted and roughly chopped
2 tablespoons extra-virgin olive oil
Grated zest of 1 lemon
Juice of ½ lemon
1 tablespoon sumac
2 teaspoons Aleppo pepper

Photo on page 73.

The shepherd's salad is all about the herbs, so don't shy away from large bunches. Some versions of this salad include feta; however, I prefer the sharpness of the crunchy vegetables and the vibrancy of herbs to show off their fresh, grassy flavour.

Aleppo pepper, also known as Turkish red pepper or *pul biber*, is commonly sold in Middle Eastern grocery shops and online.

Combine the tomatoes and salt in a large bowl. Add the cucumber and spring onions (scallions) and mix. Stir in the herbs and olives.

In a small bowl, combine the olive oil, lemon zest and juice, sumac and Aleppo pepper. Pour the dressing over the vegetables and toss to combine. Set aside for 30 minutes until the flavours have mingled.

The salad can be covered and stored in the refrigerator for up to 3 days.

SANDWICHES

L–R Hummus and Pickled Vegetable Wrap (page 82), Squash and Walnut Arayes (page 83).

BAHARAT-RUBBED MUSHROOM KEBABS

Serves 4

For the kebabs

1 x (225-g/8-oz) block halloumi, drained and soaked in cold water for 2 hours

4 portobello mushrooms, quartered

4 garlic cloves, finely chopped

1 tablespoon apple cider vinegar

1 tablespoon Baharat (page 254)

1 teaspoon salt

4 tablespoons extra-virgin olive oil, plus extra for brushing

For the spiced herb sauce

Bunch of coriander (cilantro), roughly chopped

Bunch of basil, roughly chopped

Bunch of parsley, roughly chopped

15 pitted green olives

1 garlic clove

½ teaspoon cumin seeds, toasted

¼ teaspoon ground cardamom

4 tablespoons extra-virgin olive oil

Juice from ½ lemon

1 teaspoon honey

Salt and black pepper

To serve

4 Lebanese Flatbreads (page 198), warmed

Fermented Red Cabbage (page 63), Fermented Red Onions (page 64) or pickles

Tahini, for drizzling

This is a full-flavour, deeply savoury recipe that will satisfy even the most committed meat-eaters. The mushrooms take on a smokiness as they cook, which is a great foil for the rich, salty halloumi and creamy tahini.

Baharat is a highly versatile spice blend, used in everything from seasonings to tagines. I have included a recipe for my favourite Baharat (page 254), but you can also purchase it at larger supermarkets if you're short on time.

Make the kebabs. If using wooden skewers, soak them in cold water for 30 minutes.

Pat dry the halloumi and cut it into 16 cubes. In a large bowl, combine the halloumi and mushrooms.

In a small bowl, combine the remaining kebab ingredients and mix well. Pour this marinade over the halloumi mixture. With clean hands, combine and set aside to marinate for 1 hour.

Meanwhile, make the spiced herb sauce. Combine all the ingredients in a blender or food processor and blend until smooth. Season to taste with salt and pepper. Transfer to a bowl.

Preheat the oven to 200°C/400°F/Gas Mark 6. Line a baking sheet with aluminium foil.

Skewer a piece of mushroom and halloumi onto a skewer. Repeat with 3 more of each. Place on the prepared baking sheet. Repeat with the remaining skewers and mushrooms until everything is used up.

Bake for 15 minutes. Turn, then brush with olive oil. Bake for another 15 minutes.

Serve the kebabs in flatbreads with the spiced herb sauce, pickles and a drizzle of tahini.

HUMMUS AND PICKLED VEGETABLE WRAP

Serves 2

- 2 flour tortillas
- 6 tablespoons hummus
- 1 tomato, thinly sliced
- ¼ cucumber, thinly sliced
- 2 tablespoons Fermented Beetroot and Turnips (page 65) or pickled vegetables
- ½ bunch coriander (cilantro), leaves only

Photo on page 78.

In most Middle Eastern households, a recipe like this is practically second nature. It's a five-minute, fuss-free lunch that I prepare frequently.

I just love the textural contrast of crunchy vegetables and creamy hummus encased in a hot wrap. But, by all means, go off-piste with your favourite fillings – Chilli Oil (page 257), cheese, herbs and spices would all work.

Lightly toast the tortillas in a dry frying pan or skillet over medium-high heat, until hot and charred in places.

Spread hummus on each tortilla. Arrange the vegetables and coriander (cilantro) along the centre. Fold up the bottom of each tortilla, then roll them from one side to another to form a wrap.

Serve immediately.

KA'EK EGG SANDWICH

Serves 1

- 1 egg
- 1 *Ka'ek* (page 205) or sesame bagel
- 2 tablespoons full-fat cream cheese
- 1 teaspoon Za'atar (page 254)
- ½ teaspoon Chilli Oil (page 257)
- Salt and black pepper

A traditional *ka'ek* is a self-service bakery, known for piping hot sesame breads stuffed with hard-boiled egg, chilli sauce, za'atar and cheese. When I'm preparing a family brunch, I like to mimic the self-service style of *ka'ek* bakeries. Everything is placed in the centre of the table, so guests can have as much or as little as they want of each ingredient.

Place the whole egg in a small saucepan and cover with cold water. Boil for 8 minutes.

Meanwhile, cut the *ka'ek* in half around the middle and toast until light golden. Spread cream cheese over the cut sides.

Remove the egg with a spoon, then cool under cold running water. Tap lightly on a hard surface to crack the shell, then run under cold water again for 30 seconds. This will help to separate the shell from the egg.

Peel the egg and discard the shell. Roughly chop the egg, then spread over the bottom half of the bread. Sprinkle with the za'atar and drizzle with the chilli oil. Season with salt and pepper, then finish with the top half of the bread. Serve immediately.

SQUASH AND WALNUT ARAYES

Serves 4

½ large butternut squash (about 800 g/ 1 lb 12 oz), halved lengthwise and seeded

Extra-virgin olive oil, for brushing and frying

1 teaspoon hot smoked paprika

Salt and black pepper

4 spring onions (scallions), white and light green parts thinly sliced

Small bunch of parsley, leaves only, finely chopped

2 garlic cloves, crushed

125 g/4¼ oz halloumi, grated

80 g/2¾ oz (⅔ cup) toasted walnuts, finely chopped

½ teaspoon ground cloves

½ teaspoon ground allspice

Pinch of cayenne pepper

6 pitta breads or Lebanese Flatbreads (page 198)

Garlic Tahini Sauce (page 258)

Photo on page 79.

A staple street food in the cities of Lebanon, *arayes* are pitta breads stuffed with spiced meat and onions. This moreish and satisfying vegetarian version is a revelation of flavour and texture, laced with crunchy walnuts and melting halloumi. Serve with a chopped salad for a more substantial midweek dinner.

Preheat the oven to 220°C/425°F/Gas Mark 7.

Place the squash in a roasting pan and brush with oil. Season with paprika and salt. With clean hands, rub the seasoning all over the squash and seed cavity. Season with pepper. Cover the squash with aluminium foil and roast for 25 minutes. Uncover and roast for another 20 minutes until caramelised and completely soft. (You should be able to insert a dinner knife into the flesh without resistance.) Roast for another 5–10 minutes if needed.

Using a spoon, scoop out the flesh (avoiding the skin) and transfer to a large mixing bowl. You should have about 550 g/1 lb 4 oz of squash. Add the remaining ingredients, except the flatbreads and garlic tahini sauce. Mix to combine, then season to taste with more salt and pepper.

Using a small, serrated knife, slice the flatbreads into 2 half-moons. Carefully and gently use a sawing motion to open the flatbreads like a pitta pocket. Take care not to pierce the breads as you go. Divide the filling between the opened flatbreads without overstuffing them.

Heat 3 tablespoons of oil in a large frying pan or skillet over medium heat, until it shimmers. Add the stuffed pittas, cut side down, and fry for 5 minutes. Using a rubber spatula, lay the pittas on one side. Weigh them down with a heavy pan and fry for a minute. Flip over and fry for another minute, until crisp and golden.

Plate the *arayes* and drizzle with garlic tahini sauce.

BAHARAT-SPICED VADA PAV WITH DATE AND TAMARIND CHUTNEY

Serves 6

Baharat-spiced vada pav

200 g/7 oz (2 cups plus 2 tablespoons) gram flour

1 teaspoon ground turmeric

Salt

500 g/1 lb 2 oz floury (baking) potatoes, unpeeled

1 tablespoon vegetable oil, for frying

1 red onion, finely chopped

2 mild green chillies, seeded and finely chopped

4 garlic cloves, finely chopped

1 tablespoon Baharat (page 254)

Small bunch of coriander (cilantro), leaves picked and chopped

6 burger buns, toasted

To serve

Zhug (page 257)

Arabic Garlic Sauce (page 258), vegan aioli or garlic mayonnaise

Date and Tamarind Chutney (page 202)

***Vada pav* is a popular cheap and satisfying Indian street food snack at any time of day or night. With the growing population from the Indian subcontinent in the Middle East, this variation has been given a fusion twist with the addition of baharat, a favourite spice blend of mine.**

This is a great build-your-own meal for a crowd of all ages.

Make the baharat-spiced vada pav. In a mixing bowl, combine the gram flour, turmeric and 4 teaspoons salt. Slowly whisk in 300 ml/10 fl oz (1¼ cups) warm water. Cover and set aside.

Meanwhile, scrub the potatoes and leave their skins intact. Place in a saucepan and cover with cold water. Add 1 tablespoon of salt to the water. Bring to a boil over high heat. Reduce the heat to medium-low and simmer for 20–40 minutes, until a knife can be inserted into the centre without resistance. Drain the potatoes in a colander, then set aside for 15 minutes to allow the steam to escape.

When the potatoes are cool enough to handle but still warm, pull away the skins with your fingers and discard. Transfer to a mixing bowl, then mash until smooth.

Heat the oil in a small frying pan or skillet over medium heat for 30 seconds Add the onion and sauté for 6 minutes, or until softened. Stir in the chillies and garlic and cook for 1–2 minutes. Stir in the baharat. Scrape the mixture into the bowl of potatoes, then stir in three-quarters of the coriander (cilantro). With clean hands, shape the potato mixture into balls, about 5 cm/2 inches in diameter. Place on a baking sheet lined with parchment paper and chill in the refrigerator for 30 minutes.

Heat the oil in a saucepan to a depth of 6 cm/2½ inches over medium heat. The oil is ready when a cube of bread dropped in sizzles on contact and turns golden in 30 seconds. (Alternatively, use a thermometer and heat to 160°C/325°F.) Whisk the gram flour batter until smooth. Dip the potato balls in the batter to coat, then carefully lower 4 balls into the hot oil. Using a slotted spoon, deep-fry for 3 minutes on each side, until golden brown. Using the same slotted spoon, transfer the balls to a paper towel–lined plate. Keep warm in a low oven, with the door slightly ajar. (The open door prevents the fried potatoes turning soggy.) Cook the remainder.

Add a teaspoon each of zhug, Arabic garlic sauce and chutney to the cut side of each bun. Place a couple of hot potato fritters in each bun and top with the remaining coriander.

The potato mixture can be prepared a day in advance, covered and stored in the refrigerator. The chutney can be stored in a jar in the refrigerator for up to 3 weeks.

SPICED CARROT AND CHICKPEA FALAFEL BURGERS

Makes 4

1 red onion, roughly chopped
2 garlic cloves, roughly chopped
1 teaspoon cumin seeds
1 teaspoon ground coriander
½ teaspoon paprika
½ teaspoon ground allspice
2–3 carrots, grated (1½ cups)
1 x (400-g/14-oz) can chickpeas, drained
Small bunch of coriander (cilantro), roughly chopped
Grated zest and juice of 1 lemon
Salt and black pepper
70 g/2½ oz (1 cup) breadcrumbs
1 egg, beaten
Vegetable oil, for frying

To serve

4 tablespoons Arabic Garlic Sauce (page 258)
4 burger buns, toasted
Rocket (arugula) or other salad leaves
Fermented Red Onions (page 64, optional)

Gently spiced, these burgers are a healthy and tasty way of sneaking an extra vegetable portion into barbecues or midweek dinners. They're a great thing to shape with children, although the red onions might be too strong a flavour for any little ones.

Don't be tempted to skip the refrigerator chilling time before shaping the patties – this helps them to firm up and retain their shape while they cook.

Pulse the onion and garlic together in a food processor until a rough paste forms.

Toast the cumin seeds in a dry frying pan or skillet over medium-high heat for a minute, until fragrant. Turn off the heat, then stir in the coriander, paprika and allspice. Transfer the spice mixture to the food processor. Add the carrots, chickpeas, coriander (cilantro) and lemon zest and juice. Season with salt and pepper. Blitz to form a rough paste. Season to taste with more salt and pepper. Add the breadcrumbs and egg and pulse a few times to combine.

With clean hands, shape the mixture into 4 equal patties. Place on a baking sheet lined with parchment paper, cover and chill in the refrigerator to firm up for at least 1 hour or up to 12 hours.

Heat enough oil to coat the bottom of a large frying pan or skillet over medium heat. Fry the burgers for 2–3 minutes, untouched. Flip, then fry for another 2–3 minutes, until crisp and golden.

Spread the Arabic garlic sauce on the cut side of the bottom buns. Add the patty, lettuce, fermented red onions, if using, and top buns.

Serve immediately.

NF

RED CABBAGE SHAWARMA

Serves 6

Vegetable oil, for greasing
1 x (1-kg/2 lb 4-oz) red cabbage, cut into 6 wedges through the root
2 garlic cloves, minced
1 teaspoon ground coriander
1 teaspoon ground cumin
½ teaspoon ground allspice
¼ teaspoon ground cinnamon
¼ teaspoon hot smoked paprika
1 teaspoon salt
3 tablespoons extra-virgin olive oil
1 tablespoon apple cider vinegar
1 tablespoon runny honey

To serve
Garlic Tahini Sauce (page 258)
6 Lebanese Flatbreads (page 198), warmed
Coriander (cilantro) leaves
75 g/2¾ oz feta (optional)
1 lemon, cut into wedges

Proper Middle Eastern shawarma shops are renowned for their large rotisseries of meat, thinly sliced and wrapped in flatbreads and finished with sauces, salads and pickles. I've created this rich, plant-based staple with red cabbage, which is crispy on the outside and buttery tender on the inside. The key to perfectly seasoned cabbage is the marinating time so don't be tempted to skip this step.

Grease a large baking sheet.

Arrange the red cabbage wedges on the prepared baking sheet so they are snug but do not overlap.

In a small bowl, combine the remaining ingredients and mix well. Using a pastry brush, spread half of the marinade over the cabbage working it into the leaves and layers. Reserve the remaining marinade. Cover the baking sheet with aluminium foil and set aside to marinate for 15 minutes.

Preheat the oven to 220°C/425°F/Gas Mark 7.

Keep the cabbage covered, then roast on the middle shelf for 30 minutes. Remove the foil, then turn the cabbage over. Brush over the remaining marinade and drizzle over the honey. Roast, uncovered, for another 20 minutes, until the cabbage is tender and caramelised.

Spread a tablespoon of the tahini sauce over each flatbread. Top with the cabbage, coriander (cilantro) and feta, if using. Serve immediately with the lemon wedges.

YOGURT-MARINATED TOFU SHAWARMA

Serves 4

For the pickled onion

1 red onion, thinly sliced

2 tablespoons apple cider vinegar or white wine vinegar

1 teaspoon sugar

For the shawarma

450 g/1 lb extra-firm tofu

2 tablespoons coriander seeds

2 tablespoons cumin seeds

6 garlic cloves, minced

1 tablespoon ground allspice

2 teaspoons Za'atar (page 254)

2 teaspoons hot smoked paprika

1 teaspoon ground turmeric

1 teaspoon ground ginger

1 teaspoon ground mace

1 teaspoon salt

½ teaspoon ground cinnamon

Black pepper

250 g/9 oz (1 cup plus 2 tablespoons) Greek yogurt

Juice of ½ lemon

Vegetable oil, for greasing

To serve

4 Lebanese Flatbreads (page 198), warmed

4 tablespoons Garlic Tahini Sauce (page 258)

Coriander (cilantro)

Seeds from ½ pomegranate

Pickled vegetables (optional)

Yogurt is commonly used to marinate meats and vegetables across the Levant. Whereas acidic marinades can turn the main ingredient tough and rubbery, the dairy proteins and mild acidity in yogurt keep everything tender without the risk of drying out.

Break the tofu into pieces, rather than slicing it, to create a lot of rough edges, which turn crispy when fried.

Make the pickled onion. Combine all the ingredients in a bowl and toss well. Place a smaller bowl over the onions to weigh the mixture down. Set aside.

Press the tofu between 2 layers of paper towel for 10 minutes until all the liquid is released. Break the tofu into 2-cm/¾-inch pieces. Set aside.

Toast the coriander and cumin seeds in a dry frying pan or skillet over medium heat, until fragrant. Transfer to a bowl, then add the remaining ingredients. Gently stir in the tofu until every piece is coated. Set aside to marinate for 1 hour.

Preheat the oven to 220°C/425°F/Gas Mark 7. Lightly grease a baking sheet with oil.

Spread out the tofu and yogurt mixture onto the prepared baking sheet in an even layer. Bake for 13 minutes. Gently turn the pieces, then bake for another 12 minutes, until they're crispy and golden in places.

Plate the flatbreads, then top with the tofu and pickled onions. Drizzle with garlic tahini sauce and finish with the coriander (cilantro), pomegranate seeds and pickled vegetables, if using.

SWEET AND SOUR AUBERGINE SLIDERS

Don't let the burger buns fool you, they're just a vehicle for the smoky aubergine (eggplant), crunchy and sharp red cabbage and salty halloumi. All the elements could be served together as a salad, but they are somehow more delicious sandwiched between a soft white bun.

Serves 4

For the salad

½ red cabbage, thinly sliced with a mandoline
Small bunch of dill, leaves only, chopped
3 tablespoons sesame seeds, toasted
½ teaspoon salt
2 tablespoons extra-virgin olive oil
1 tablespoon Pomegranate Molasses (page 256)
Juice of 1 lime

For the sliders

2 large aubergines (eggplants)
2 tablespoons extra-virgin olive oil
1 onion, finely chopped
Salt
2 tomatoes, roughly chopped
3½ tablespoons frozen peas
1 teaspoon ground cumin
1 teaspoon ground coriander
1 teaspoon Aleppo pepper
½ teaspoon ground cardamom
Pinch of chilli flakes
250 g/9 oz halloumi, cut into 1-cm/½-inch slices
2 tablespoons runny honey
4 burger buns, toasted

Make the salad. Combine all the ingredients in a bowl. With clean hands, scrunch them together for 3–5 minutes to work the salt and pomegranate molasses into the cabbage. Set aside.

Make the sliders. Preheat the grill (broiler) or a griddle pan over high heat for 5 minutes. Add the aubergines (eggplants), turning every few minutes or so, until the skins are charred and the aubergines are collapsing. Set aside to cool in a colander.

Heat the oil in a large frying pan or skillet over medium heat. Add the onion and a pinch of salt and sauté for 8 minutes, until soft and translucent. Add the tomatoes, peas, cumin, coriander, Aleppo pepper, cardamom and chilli flakes. Stir for 2 minutes, until fragrant. Reduce the heat to low and cook for another 8 minutes, until the tomatoes have completely softened.

Meanwhile, peel the aubergine skins and discard. Roughly chop the flesh, then add them to the pan. Season with salt. Cook for 10–12 minutes, until the mixture is completely combined and the aubergine appears mashed. Reduce the heat to low and keep warm.

In another frying pan, pan-fry the halloumi over medium heat for 3 minutes on each side, until golden and slightly crispy. Drizzle with honey.

Arrange the open buns on plates. Add a couple of halloumi pieces to each bun, then top with a spoonful of aubergine mixture and cabbage salad. Serve immediately.

Leftover cabbage salad can be covered and stored in the refrigerator for up to 3 days.

BRUNCH

L–R Beetroot Koftes (page 105), Tomato and Mint Mezze (page 173).

LEBANESE HERB OMELETTE

Serves 4

For the tahini sauce

1 garlic clove, crushed

¼ teaspoon ground cumin

¼ teaspoon salt, plus extra to taste

4 tablespoons tahini

Juice of ½ lemon, plus extra to taste

For the omelette

6 eggs

Bunch of spring onions (scallions), thinly sliced diagonally

Bunch of parsley, finely chopped

½ bunch mint, leaves only, chopped

4 tablespoons plain (all-purpose) flour

1 teaspoon ground coriander

Salt and black pepper

Olive oil, for frying

Parsley and mint leaves, to garnish

This easy omelette (also known as *ejeh*) is perfect for breakfast or lunch alongside a pitta or flatbread and sliced tomatoes. There are many variations across Lebanon, but fresh herbs are always the star. This version is made with spring onions (scallions), parsley and mint but feel free to experiment with your favourite herbs.

The addition of flour bridges the gap between pancakes and omelettes. It can be replaced with a gluten-free flour if you wish.

Make the tahini sauce. In a small bowl, combine all the ingredients. (It will seize and thicken as the lemon reacts with the tahini.) Add up to 4 tablespoons of water, a tablespoon at a time, mixing after each addition until the mixture has the consistency of thick yogurt. Season to taste with more salt and lemon.

Make the omelette. In a medium bowl, gently whisk the eggs to break up the yolks. Add the spring onions (scallions) and herbs and whisk again to combine. Sieve (sift) the flour over the egg mixture, add the coriander and mix until smooth. Season with salt and pepper.

Heat enough oil to thinly coat a large heavy frying pan or skillet over medium heat. Ladle the egg mixture into the pan and pan-fry for 2–3 minutes on each side, until golden. The pancakes should measure about 10 cm/4 inches. Transfer to a plate. Repeat with the remaining batter.

Serve warm with tahini sauce and garnished with the herbs.

LITTLE RICE BREAKFAST BUNS WITH HARISSA EGGS

Serves 8

For the buns

250 g/9 oz (1 cup plus 3 tablespoons) uncooked basmati rice

¼ teaspoon fenugreek seeds

100 g/3½ oz (½ cup plus 1 tablespoon) ground rice

125 g/4¼ oz (⅔ cup) cooked basmati rice

3 tablespoons desiccated coconut

400 ml/14 fl oz (1⅔ cups) full-fat coconut milk

½ teaspoon salt

3 tablespoons melted coconut oil

½ teaspoon bicarbonate of soda (baking soda)

For the eggs

2–3 tablespoons vegetable oil or ghee, for frying

8 eggs

8 teaspoons Rose Harissa (page 256)

Zhug (page 257), to serve (optional)

Coriander (cilantro) leaves, to garnish

Somewhere between a Kerala-style rice pancake (*appam*) and a breakfast muffin, these little buns are crowd-pleasers at brunch. Just be sure to rein in the harissa for young children.

They require a bit of time and patience, but the results are well worth the effort and wait. And if you want to stretch out the batter, keep it covered and refrigerated for up to a week.

Make the buns. Soaked the uncooked rice in 500 ml/17 fl oz (2 cups plus 1 tablespoon) of cold water for 4 hours. Drain.

Combine the drained rice and remaining ingredients, except the melted coconut oil and the bicarbonate of soda (baking soda), in a high-speed blender. Add 375 ml/13 fl oz (1⅔ cups) of cold water and blend for 5 minutes, until smooth. Cover with a clean dish towel (you want some air flow to the batter) and set aside to ferment overnight. Alternatively, leave covered and refrigerate the batter for up to a week.

Preheat the oven to 220°C/425°F/Gas Mark 7. Grease a 12-cup muffin pan with 1 tablespoon of the melted coconut oil. Place the pan in the oven for 3 minutes, until the oil is heated.

Uncover the rice batter, then whisk in the bicarbonate of soda until smooth. Using a ladle, pour batter into each cup (a bit like preparing a Yorkshire pudding), leaving 2 mm/1⁄16 inch of space at the top of each cup. This allows the batter to rise.

Bake for 10 minutes, until crisp, golden and domed in the centre. Using a small rubber spatula, release the buns and keep warm. Repeat with the remaining oil and batter.

Make the eggs. Once the final buns are in the oven, heat the vegetable oil or ghee in a large frying pan or skillet over medium-high heat until sizzling. Add the eggs and pan-fry for 2 minutes, until the whites are set and the edges are crispy. If necessary, work in batches to avoid overcrowding.

Place 3 or 4 little buns on each serving plate. Top with a fried egg, harissa and zhug, if using, and garnish with the coriander (cilantro) leaves.

SEMOLINA PORRIDGE WITH CHARRED CHILLI CORN

Serves 4

3 tablespoons ghee or olive oil
1 onion, finely chopped
Salt and black pepper
125 g/4¼ oz (¾ cup) coarse semolina (farina)
½ teaspoon ground cumin
4 ears corn, kernels shaved off
1 mild red chilli, finely chopped
1 teaspoon black mustard seeds
Juice of 1 lime
75 g/2¾ oz crumbled feta, to garnish (optional)
Fermented Red Cabbage (page 63), to serve

Semolina is a coarsely milled wheat that's commonly used to make couscous and pasta. I also love it as a comforting porridge – its nutty, creamy flavour pairs so well with sweetcorn. I use fresh corn on the cob for this recipe, but you could make it with a 400-g/14-oz can of drained sweetcorn.

Heat 1 tablespoon of ghee or olive oil in a saucepan over medium heat. Add the onion and a pinch of salt and sauté for 8 minutes, until softened and translucent but not coloured. Stir in the semolina (farina) and cumin and toast for 2 minutes, stirring continuously. Slowly pour in 700 ml/24 fl oz (scant 3 cups) boiling water and mix until smooth. Reduce the heat to low and gently simmer for 20 minutes, until the porridge is no longer grainy. Season to taste with salt and pepper.

Meanwhile, heat the remaining 2 tablespoons of ghee in a large frying pan or skillet over high heat. Add the corn and sauté for 8–10 minutes, until the corn is tender and charred in places. Add the chilli and mustard seeds and sauté for another minute, until the mustard seeds start to pop. Remove from the heat and squeeze over the lime.

Divide the porridge among warm bowls. Top with the corn, feta, if using, and fermented red cabbage. Serve immediately.

SWEET PORRIDGE

Serves 2

2 tablespoons butter
125 g/4¼ oz (¾ cup) coarse semolina (farina)
2 tablespoons desiccated coconut
1 teaspoon ground cardamom
Pinch of saffron strands
525 ml/17½ fl oz (2¼ cups) milk
1 x (395-g/14-oz) can condensed milk
1 tablespoon rosewater
1 tablespoon honey
1 teaspoon edible dried rose petals
1 teaspoon slivered pistachios
Fresh fruit or compote, to serve (optional)

Inspired by the Omani dish *khabees*, this sweet porridge has a delicately spiced fragrance and sunny flavours, and is so uplifting that it will brighten your day. Best of all, it can be served at breakfast or as a dessert.

Melt the butter in a medium saucepan over low heat. Add the semolina (farina) and stir for 5 minutes to gently toast the semolina. Stir in the coconut, cardamom and saffron and cook for another minute, until fragrant.

Pour in the milk, condensed milk, rosewater and honey. Gently simmer for 18–20 minutes, stirring occasionally, until the mixture has thickened and holds together.

Transfer into warm bowls, then garnish with the rose petals and pistachios. Serve with fresh fruit or compote, if using.

BEETROOT KOFTES

Serves 4

2 tablespoons neutral oil, for frying
1 red onion, finely chopped
Salt and black pepper
2 garlic cloves, grated
2 teaspoons cumin seeds
1 teaspoon ground coriander
1 teaspoon sweet smoked paprika
½ teaspoon cayenne pepper
2 beetroot (beets), peeled and coarsely grated
1 x (400-g/14-oz) can cannellini or butter (lima) beans, drained
50 g/1¾ oz (⅔ cup) breadcrumbs
70 g/2½ oz (generous ½ cup) toasted walnuts
1 teaspoon dried mint
2 tablespoons tahini

To serve
Lebanese Flatbreads (page 198)
Salad leaves
Garlic Tahini Sauce (page 258)

Photo on page 96.

Meatballs, koftes, polpette . . . whatever language you speak, there's likely to be a recipe with a similar idea in another. In the Middle East, koftes are made with beef or lamb and a blend of spices. I love this beetroot (beet) version, which is at once light and super satisfying.

Heat the oil in a large frying pan or skillet over medium heat. Add the onion and a pinch of salt and sauté for 8 minutes, until soft and translucent. Add the garlic and spices and sauté for another 2 minutes, until fragrant. Stir in the beetroot (beets) and beans and cook until piping hot.

Transfer the mixture to the bowl of a food processor. Add the breadcrumbs, walnuts, mint and tahini. Season well with salt and pepper. Process until the mixture is almost smooth. Transfer to a bowl, then set aside to cool. Chill in the refrigerator for at least 4 hours, or overnight.

Preheat the oven to 220°C/425°F/Gas Mark 7. Line a baking sheet with parchment paper.

Roll 50 g/1¾ oz of the dough between clean palms to form an oval. Gently pinch and roll to form a point at each end. Place on the prepared baking sheet. Repeat with the remaining dough. Bake for 30 minutes, until the surface of each kofte is dry and beginning to crack in places.

Serve the koftes with flatbread, salad and garlic tahini sauce.

SPICED SCRAMBLED EGGS

Serves 4

3 tablespoons olive oil

2 Turkish green peppers, finely chopped (see Note)

Small bunch of spring onions (scallions), white and light green parts thinly sliced

1 teaspoon dried oregano

¼ teaspoon cayenne pepper

¼ teaspoon ground coriander

Salt and black pepper

1 x (400-g/14-oz) can chopped tomatoes

6 eggs

To serve

4 slices toast or Lebanese flatbreads (page 198)

4 tablespoons Greek yogurt (optional)

Aleppo pepper, for sprinkling

Small bunch of parsley, roughly chopped

Small bunch of dill, roughly chopped

1 tablespoon chopped chives

Extra-virgin olive oil, for drizzling

The flavours in this punchy breakfast meal aren't dissimilar to shakshouka, the Middle Eastern baked egg dish that has taken over trendy brunch menus across the globe. I find this dish far more interesting, because the eggs are folded into the spicy tomato sauce.

Be generous with the olive oil when finishing the dish – the richness makes it special.

Heat the olive oil in a large non-stick frying pan or skillet over medium heat. Add the Turkish pepper, spring onions (scallions), oregano, cayenne pepper, coriander and a pinch of salt and pepper. Reduce the heat to medium-low and sauté for 8–10 minutes, until softened.

Stir in the tomatoes and increase the heat to medium. Sauté for another 4–5 minutes, until the colour has deepened and thickened. Transfer half of the mixture to a plate. Reduce the heat to low.

Gently whisk the eggs with a fork in a bowl just to break the yolk, so the egg still has distinct yellow streaks among the transparent white. Add the eggs to the pan and fold it into the mixture, until it's just set. Add the remaining tomato mixture and stir to combine.

Place the toast or flatbread on serving plates. Top with a dollop of yogurt, if using, a sprinkling of Aleppo pepper and chopped herbs. Generously drizzle with extra-virgin olive oil and serve.

Note

The Turkish green pepper, or *sivri biber*, is commonly served alongside plates of roast or grilled meats at every Turkish restaurant. It's a long, slender and light green pepper with a mild-medium heat. If you cannot find it, replace it with 1 green pepper and 1 green chilli.

SPICED POTATO CAKES

Serves 6

750 g/1 lb 10 oz floury (baking) potatoes, scrubbed and unpeeled

Salt and black pepper

2 tablespoons ghee, plus extra for frying

1 red onion, finely chopped

4 garlic cloves, finely chopped

Small bunch of coriander (cilantro), leaves only, chopped

50 g/1¾ oz (scant 1 cup) fresh breadcrumbs

1 tablespoon ground cumin

1 tablespoon ground coriander

1 teaspoon ground turmeric

1 teaspoon Baharat (page 254)

3 eggs, beaten

Although Morocco is not included in the Levant region, we share many of the same spices and flavours. These little patties (*maakouda*) are inspired by my travels in the area, and could be related to Jewish latkes, as they both require the starch to be drawn out of the potatoes to create the crisp-edged cakes. I make a big batch of these for brunch and serve them with eggs and fresh tomatoes.

Place the potatoes in a large saucepan and cover with double the volume of cold water. Add 1 tablespoon of salt. Bring to a boil, then reduce the heat to medium-low and simmer gently for 18–20 minutes, until the potatoes are soft enough to be pierced with a knife but before they become soft like room-temperature butter. Drain the potatoes, then rinse under cold running water.

When cool enough to handle, peel the potatoes. Grate them into a large mixing bowl. Add 1 teaspoon of salt and rub the salt into the potatoes for 3–5 minutes, until the volume of liquid in the bowl is a third of that of the potatoes. (The salt helps to draw water out of the potatoes.)

With clean hands, grab a handful of potatoes and squeeze out as much of the water as possible. (You may need to do this in batches.) Transfer the squeezed potatoes to the centre of a clean dish towel and squeeze again over the sink to extract as much of the water as possible. Transfer the dried potatoes to a large bowl. Repeat with the remaining potatoes.

Heat the ghee in a frying pan or skillet over medium heat. Add the red onion and sauté for 6 minutes, until softened. Add the garlic and sauté for another minute. Transfer this mixture to the bowl with the potatoes. Wipe the pan with paper towels and set aside.

Add the remaining ingredients to the potato mixture and stir to combine. Line a baking sheet with paper towels.

Heat enough ghee to coat the bottom of the same pan over medium heat. Add a heaped tablespoon of potato mixture, pressing down with the back of the spoon to flatten the patty. Add a few more, taking care not to overcrowd the pan. Pan-fry for 3–4 minutes on each side, until crisp and golden all over. Transfer the potato cakes to the prepared pan and keep warm in a low oven. Repeat with the remaining potato cakes.

Serve immediately.

ZA'ATAR TOMATO TOAST

Serves 2

4 very ripe tomatoes
Salt and black pepper
4 slices bread, or 8 slices baguette, toasted
1 garlic clove, cut in half
¼ teaspoon Aleppo pepper
1 teaspoon Za'atar (page 254)
½ lemon
Extra-virgin olive oil, for drizzling

My inspiration for this dish came after a conversation with a Spanish friend who has *pan con tomate* most days, a garlicky tomato bread served everywhere from Galicia to Barcelona.

I like to make this when I have a glut of tomatoes in the summer. This makes a lovely light breakfast or brunch, alongside a cup of Arabic coffee.

Grate the tomatoes into a bowl and discard the skins. Season with a generous pinch of salt and a little pepper. The tomato can be covered and stored in the refrigerator for up to 4 hours.

Arrange the toast on serving plates. Rub the cut sides of the garlic clove over the top side of the toast. Spoon over the seasoned tomatoes, then sprinkle over the Aleppo pepper and za'atar. Grate the lemon zest over the toasts. (The juice can be reserved for something else, such as dressing or a hot lemon tea.) Drizzle with extra-virgin olive oil.

Serve immediately.

SOUPS & STEWS

L–R Cumin Squash Stew with Cauliflower and Pine Nut Crumble (page 129), Lebanese Chickpea and Garlic Stew with Quick Pickled Radishes (page 122).

SPICED CHICKPEAS IN BROTH WITH WHIPPED TAHINI YOGURT

Serves 8

For the chickpeas

400 g/14 oz (1¾ cups) dried chickpeas (see Note)

1 teaspoon fine salt

1 teaspoon bicarbonate of soda (baking soda)

For the stew

4 tablespoons extra-virgin olive oil, plus extra for finishing

2 white onions, finely chopped

6 garlic cloves, thinly sliced

3 fresh bay leaves

5 cardamom pods

1 star anise

1 cinnamon stick

1 tablespoon ground cumin

1 tablespoon ground coriander

1 tablespoon Aleppo pepper or 1 teaspoon chilli flakes

2 tomatoes, roughly chopped

½ teaspoon bicarbonate of soda (baking soda)

Pared zest of 1 lemon

For the tahini yogurt

200 g/7 oz (scant 1 cup) Greek yogurt

3 tablespoons tahini

1 teaspoon nigella seeds

Juice of 1 lemon

Salt and black pepper

Note

In a pinch, you could use 2 x (600-g/1 lb 5-oz) jars of chickpeas. (You want to avoid the canned versions, which can sometimes be mealy.) Bypass the soaking instructions and add only 750 ml/25 fl oz (3 cups) of water to make the broth.

Many people I know find cooking chickpeas from their dried state either tedious or, at worst, overwhelming. Sure, it requires a little forward-thinking, but you'll be rewarded with tender chickpeas that absorb all the aromatic flavour from their cooking broth.

Prepare the chickpeas. In a large bowl, combine all the ingredients. Add 3 times the volume of water, then set aside to soak overnight.

The next day, make the stew. Heat the oil in a large saucepan over medium heat, until it shimmers. Add the onions and 1 teaspoon of salt and sauté for 8 minutes, until soft. Add the garlic, bay leaves and spices and sauté for 2 minutes, until deeply fragrant. Stir in the tomatoes.

Drain, then rinse the chickpeas. Add the chickpeas, bicarbonate of soda (baking soda), 1 teaspoon of salt, lemon zest and 1.5 litres/50 fl oz (6¼ cups) of water. Bring to a boil. Reduce the heat to medium-low and simmer for 30 minutes–1½ hours, until the chickpeas are very tender. Skim off any froth from the surface and discard.

Meanwhile, make the tahini yogurt. Whisk all the ingredients in a bowl. Season with salt and pepper, then chill in the refrigerator.

Season the broth with salt and pepper. Ladle the chickpeas into warm bowls, top with a spoonful of the tahini yogurt and drizzle with olive oil. Serve.

The chickpeas can be stored in an airtight container in the refrigerator for up to 5 days.

BRAISED CHICKPEAS WITH SUMAC GREENS

Serves 6

For the chickpeas

350 g/12 oz (1½ cups) dried chickpeas

1 teaspoon fine salt

1 teaspoon bicarbonate of soda (baking soda)

For the stew

5 tablespoons extra-virgin olive oil

1 head garlic, cloves separated, peeled and finely chopped

3 fresh bay leaves

½ teaspoon black pepper

2 teaspoons Aleppo pepper or ½ teaspoon chilli flakes

½ teaspoon bicarbonate of soda (baking soda)

1 tablespoon salt

150 g/5½ oz cold butter, cut into cubes

140 g/5 oz (1⅔ cups) finely grated Parmesan-style cheese

For the sumac greens

1 tablespoon extra-virgin olive oil

150 g/5½ oz cabbage, kale or spinach, shredded

2 teaspoons sumac

Salt and black pepper

Juice of ½ lemon

This is the only recipe in the book for which I insist you prepare dried chickpeas. When doing so, the starchy cooking water magically thickens when you stir in the cheese – you won't achieve a similar result with canned or jarred chickpeas.

I use a microplane to grate the Parmesan-style cheese as fine as possible. You may be tempted to switch to a larger size, but the small pieces of cheese melt evenly into the soup.

Prepare the chickpeas. In a large bowl, combine all the ingredients. Add 3 times the volume of water, then set aside to soak overnight.

The next day, make the stew. Preheat the oven to 160°C/325°F/ Gas Mark 3.

Heat 5 tablespoons of the oil in a large casserole (Dutch oven) over medium-low heat. Add the garlic, bay leaves, black pepper and Aleppo pepper and sauté for 2 minutes, until deeply fragrant and the garlic begins to turn golden.

Drain and rinse the chickpeas, then add to the pan. Pour in 1.2 litres/40 fl oz (5 cups) water. Stir in the bicarbonate of soda (baking soda) and salt. Cover, then bring to a boil. Stir again, then cover. Transfer to the oven and cook for 2 hours, until very tender.

In 8 additions, add the butter cubes and Parmesan-style cheese, stirring after every addition, until the cheese is melted and the braising liquid is thick and emulsified. Keep warm over low heat.

Make the sumac greens. Heat the oil in a saucepan over medium heat. Add the greens and cover to steam and wilt. This will take anywhere between a minute for spinach and 5–6 minutes for cabbage and kale. Uncover, then stir to coat the leaves in the oil. Stir in the sumac, then add a pinch of salt and pepper. Squeeze over the lemon juice, then season to taste.

Ladle the cheesy chickpeas into warm bowls. Top with the sumac greens. Serve immediately.

The chickpeas will keep covered in a sealed container in the refrigerator for up to a week.

MOLOKHIA STEW

Serves 6

2 tablespoons coriander seeds
½ teaspoon black peppercorns
2 tablespoons extra-virgin olive oil
6 garlic cloves, finely chopped
475 ml/16 fl oz (2 cups) vegetable stock
Pinch of bicarbonate of soda (baking soda)
400 g/14 oz frozen chopped molokhia leaves, rinsed well
1 teaspoon salt
Juice of 1 lemon
Basmati rice or Lebanese Flatbreads (page 198), to serve
6 tablespoons crispy onions, to serve

Molokhia, a leaf from the jute mallow plant, is ubiquitous across the Levantine. It is typically served in a deep green soup with coriander (cilantro) and lots of garlic over rice – an inexpensive street food staple with a slightly unctuous (some may say slimy) texture, not unlike okra. Rinse the leaves first to prevent them from becoming too slick in the pan.

Molokhia leaves can be purchased frozen from Middle Eastern shops and in some larger supermarkets.

Add the coriander seeds and peppercorns to a dry frying pan or skillet. Toast over medium heat for a minute, stirring occasionally, until deeply fragrant. (Watch carefully to prevent them from going too dark and burning; otherwise, they will taste very bitter.) Using a spice grinder or pestle and mortar, grind the seeds to a fine powder.

Heat the oil in a large saucepan over medium heat. Add the garlic and sauté for 30 seconds, until the garlic begins to turn golden. Add the stock and bicarbonate of soda (baking soda) and bring to a simmer. Add the frozen molokhia and gently stir, until it is completely thawed and mixed in. Reduce the heat to medium-low and simmer for 15 minutes. Stir in the salt and cook for another 3 minutes. Remove from the heat, then stir in the lemon juice.

Place the basmati rice or flatbread in individual serving bowls. Ladle over the stew, then top with the crispy onions.

LEBANESE CHICKPEA AND GARLIC STEW WITH QUICK PICKLED RADISHES

Serves 4 as a starter, or as part of a mezze spread

For the stew

225 g/8 oz (1 cup) chickpeas

2 teaspoons salt

1 teaspoon bicarbonate of soda (baking soda)

3 bay leaves

3 black peppercorns

2 tablespoons ghee or olive oil

3 garlic cloves, crushed

1 teaspoon ground cumin

¼ teaspoon cayenne pepper

2 tablespoons pine nuts

Grated zest and juice of ½ lemon

For the pickled radishes

6 radishes, thinly sliced

1 tablespoon red wine vinegar

2 teaspoons sugar

½ teaspoon coriander seeds

¼ teaspoon salt

Photo on page 115.

Chickpeas are as common in Lebanon as bread, and this dish is the unifying fuel for blue- and white-collar workers on their way to work. In Beirut, they often sit side by side, slurping a bowl of this stew, known as *balila,* and enjoying it alongside a hot Arabic coffee. This beloved dish can also be served as part of a hot mezze dinner or more elaborate meals.

The pickled radishes aren't strictly traditional, but they look so pretty with their bright pink skins against the chickpeas. The longer you leave the pickles, the pinker they will become, so bear that in mind if you're aiming for a striking look.

In a large bowl, combine the chickpeas, 1 teaspoon of salt and ½ teaspoon of bicarbonate of soda (baking soda). Add 3 times the volume of water, then set aside to soak overnight.

The next day, drain the chickpeas, then rinse in a colander under cold running water. In a saucepan, combine the chickpeas, 1 bay leaf, the peppercorns, the remaining 1 teaspoon of salt and ½ teaspoon of bicarbonate of soda (baking soda). Add 3 times the volume of water and bring to a boil. Reduce the heat to medium, then simmer for 1–2 hours, until the chickpeas are very tender.

Meanwhile, make the pickled radishes. Combine all the ingredients in a bowl. With clean hands, scrunch together to work the spices and sugar into the radishes. Cover with a clean jar to weight it down, then set aside for 30 minutes–2 hours.

Heat 1 tablespoon of the ghee or oil in a frying pan or skillet over medium-high heat. Add the garlic and the remaining 2 bay leaves and sauté for a minute, until fragrant. Remove from the heat.

Drain the chickpeas, reserving 100 ml/3½ fl oz (scant ½ cup) of the cooking liquid.

Return the garlic to the heat. Stir in the cumin, cayenne pepper, chickpeas and the reserved cooking liquid. Cook over low heat for 15 minutes, until the flavours have mingled.

Meanwhile, heat the remaining tablespoon of ghee in a small frying pan or skillet over medium heat. Add the pine nuts and sauté for a minute, until golden all over. Remove the chickpeas from the heat. Stir in the lemon zest and juice.

Transfer the mixture to a serving bowl and top with the pine nuts. Drain the radishes on paper towels, then sprinkle over the chickpeas. Serve.

To prepare this ahead, prepare the chickpeas and radishes separately, then combine them when ready to serve.

The chickpeas can be covered and stored in the refrigerator for up to 5 days.

LENTIL SOUP WITH TAMARIND AND GREENS

Serves 6

For the lentil soup
4 tablespoons extra-virgin olive oil
2 red onions, thinly sliced
1½ teaspoons salt
6 garlic cloves, finely chopped
2 mild green chillies, finely chopped
2 cardamom pods
1 teaspoon cumin seeds
1 teaspoon coriander seeds
1 teaspoon mild curry powder
1 tablespoon tomato purée (paste)
150 g/5½ oz (scant ¾ cup) dried brown lentils
1 x (400-g/14-oz) bag spinach leaves, well rinsed
3 tablespoons tamarind paste
Large bunch of coriander (cilantro), roughly chopped
6 tablespoons Greek yogurt, to garnish
2–3 tablespoons crispy onions, to garnish

For the spiced oil
4 tablespoons extra-virgin olive oil
4 garlic cloves, thinly sliced
1 teaspoon ground turmeric
¼ teaspoon chilli flakes

Photo on page 133.

Tamarind has a pleasing sour and fruity flavour, making this kitchen staple a great stand-in for lemon. If you can't find tamarind, try adding lime juice instead for a sharp lift.

This wonderful main course can be veganised by using plant-based yogurt.

Heat the oil in a saucepan over medium heat. Add the onions and ½ teaspoon of the salt and sauté for 15 minutes, until the onions are soft and start to caramelise. Stir in the garlic, chillies, spices and tomato purée (paste) and cook for 2 minutes. Add the lentils, the remaining salt and 1 litre/34 fl oz (4¼ cups) of hot water. Cover and simmer for 15 minutes.

Add the spinach. Leave untouched (do not stir), cover and steam for 7 minutes. Stir to combine. Stir in the tamarind paste and coriander (cilantro). Keep warm over low heat.

Make the spiced oil. Heat the oil in a frying pan or skillet over medium heat, until it shimmers. Add the garlic, turmeric and chilli flakes. Sauté for 2 minutes, until the garlic is crispy.

Ladle the soup into bowls. Top with a dollop of Greek yogurt, a drizzle of spiced oil and crispy onions.

The soup can be covered and stored in the refrigerator for 3 days.

RED LENTIL SOUP WITH SPICED CAULIFLOWER

Serves 6

For the soup

200 g/7 oz (¾ cup plus 2 tablespoons) red lentils

75 g/2¾ oz (⅓ cup) short-grain rice

4 tablespoons neutral oil

2 onions, finely chopped

2 carrots, finely chopped

2 sticks celery, finely chopped

2 tomatoes, diced

2 fresh bay leaves

2 teaspoons ground cumin

1 teaspoon ground turmeric

1 teaspoon sweet paprika

2 litres/1¾ quarts unsalted/low salt vegetable stock

100 g/3½ oz spinach or Swiss chard, shredded

Juice of 2 lemons

Salt and black pepper

1 tablespoon cumin seeds

1 tablespoon sesame seeds

Parsley leaves, to garnish (optional)

For the cauliflower

1 x (700-g/1 lb 9-oz) cauliflower, cut into 2-cm/¾-inch florets

1½ teaspoons ras-el-hanout

¼ teaspoon salt

2 tablespoons neutral oil

This soup is on the right side of warming without being overwhelmingly spicy – and a favourite with every generation of my family. Traditionally, the silky-smooth soup is served on its own, occasionally with strained yogurt on top, but I like the contrast of nutty roasted cauliflower, which is entirely optional.

Naturally vegan and gluten-free, it's a fantastic soup to serve to a group with different dietary requirements.

Make the soup. Combine the lentils and rice in a bowl. Cover with 3 times the volume of cold water. Set aside.

Preheat the oven to 220°C/425°F/Gas Mark 7.

Heat 2 tablespoons of the oil in a large saucepan over medium heat. Add the onions, carrots, celery and 2 teaspoons of salt. Sauté for 10 minutes, until the onions are soft and translucent. Reduce the heat to low and cook for 15 minutes, until the vegetables are caramelised.

Stir in the tomatoes, bay leaves and spices. Reduce the heat to low and cook for 5 minutes, until the spices are toasted and fragrant.

Drain the lentils and rice through a fine-mesh sieve, then rinse well under cold running water. Add to the pan, then pour in the stock. Bring to a boil, then reduce the heat to medium-low. Cover and simmer for 25 minutes, until the lentils and rice are completely soft.

Meanwhile, make the cauliflower. In a roasting pan, combine all the ingredients and mix well. Spread out the cauliflower, spacing out the florets. Roast for 20 minutes, until golden and crispy.

Remove the saucepan from the heat. Discard the bay leaves. Using an immersion blender, blend the soup until smooth. Heat over low heat. Stir in the spinach or chard and cook for 2 minutes, until wilted. Add the lemon juice. Season to taste with salt and pepper.

Heat the remaining 2 tablespoons of oil in a frying pan or skillet over medium-high heat, until it shimmers. Add the cumin and sesame seeds and toast for 30 seconds.

Ladle the soup into warm bowls. Top with the roasted cauliflower and parsley, if using, and a drizzle of the spiced oil.

The soup will keep in an airtight container in the refrigerator for 1 week or in the freezer for 6 months.

NF

MIDDLE EASTERN NOODLE SOUP

Serves 6

2 tablespoons extra-virgin olive oil
2 onions, thinly sliced
Salt
3 tablespoons tomato purée (paste)
2 garlic cloves, thinly sliced
1 teaspoon coriander seeds
½ teaspoon Aleppo pepper
¼ teaspoon ground cinnamon
2 tomatoes, roughly chopped
150 g/5½ oz broken vermicelli, plus 50 g/1¾ oz for frying
1 dried black lime
1.75 litres/60 fl oz (7½ cups) hot vegetable stock
2 tablespoons ghee
1 cardamom pod, split with the side of a knife
2 teaspoons cumin seeds
2 teaspoons nigella seeds

To serve

Seeds from ½ pomegranate
6 sprigs dill, leaves only
2 tablespoons tahini

Whenever I feel under the weather or need comforting, I turn to a noodle soup. Without requiring much effort, it leaves me feeling satisfied and full of goodness.

I add a spiced ghee mixture to this soup, just before serving, which is a technique known as 'tempering'. Whole spices are sizzled in hot fat, then added at the end of a dish to extract as much flavour from the spices as possible. It injects a punchy flavour boost to soups, stews and curries.

Heat the oil in a deep saucepan over medium heat, until it shimmers. Add the onions and 1 teaspoon of salt and sauté over medium heat for 20 minutes, until soft, jammy and caramelised. Add the tomato purée (paste), garlic and spices and sauté for another minute, until fragrant. Stir in the tomatoes and a pinch of salt. Cook for another 8 minutes, stirring occasionally, until the tomatoes break down and the mixture resembles a rough paste.

Add the vermicelli, dried lime and stock. Bring to a boil, then reduce the heat to medium-low. Simmer for 10 minutes, until the soup has thickened and the noodles are cooked through. If the soup is too thick, loosen it up with a little water.

Heat the ghee in a saucepan over medium heat for a minute. Add the cardamom, cumin and nigella seeds, which should all sizzle immediately. Fry for another minute, then pour the mixture into the soup.

Toast the extra vermicelli in a dry frying pan or skillet over medium-high heat until all the strands are golden. Remove from the heat.

Ladle the hot soup into bowls. Top with the pomegranate seeds, fried vermicelli and dill. Drizzle with the tahini.

SPICED LENTIL AND PINE NUT CURRY

Serves 4–6

3 tablespoons extra-virgin olive oil
2 onions, thinly sliced
Salt and black pepper
4 garlic cloves, crushed
2 bay leaves
4 cardamom pods
2 teaspoons ground coriander
1 teaspoon ground turmeric
½ teaspoon allspice
¼ teaspoon ground cinnamon
4 carrots, cut into 1-cm/½-inch dice
2 tablespoons tomato purée (paste)
1 x (400-g/14-oz) can green lentils, drained
1 x (400-g/14-oz) can chopped tomatoes
2 dried black limes, pierced with a skewer
50 g/1¾ oz (scant ½ cup) toasted pine nuts
Small bunch of coriander (cilantro), leaves only
100 ml/3½ fl oz (scant ½ cup) coconut cream
Bunch of spring onions (scallions), white and light green parts only, thinly sliced and soaked in cold water, to garnish
1 lime, cut into wedges, to serve
Cooked rice, Lebanese Flatbreads (page 198) or Chickpea Pancakes (page 46), to serve

This rich and unique curry, made with buttery lentils and toasted pine nuts, is such a flavour revelation. Although it may look like a long list of ingredients, many of these things are likely to be in the cupboard already.

Heat the oil in a large frying pan or skillet over medium heat. Add the onions and ½ teaspoon of salt and sauté for 8 minutes, until soft and translucent. Add the garlic and bay leaves and cook for another minute, until intensely fragrant.

Reduce the heat to medium-low. Stir in the spices and 1 tablespoon of water. Add the carrots and tomato purée (paste) and stir to combine. Add the lentils and canned tomatoes. Fill the can with hot water, then add this to the pan. Add the dried black limes. Bring the pan to a boil, then reduce the heat to medium-low.

Using a pestle and mortar, crush the pine nuts until it forms a smooth paste. Stir it into the mixture. Cover and gently simmer for 20 minutes, until the carrots are tender. Uncover and simmer for another 10 minutes, stirring occasionally, until thickened.

Discard the black limes and bay leaves. Season to taste with salt and pepper. Sprinkle over the coriander (cilantro) leaves and drizzle with the coconut cream.

Garnish the curry with spring onions (scallions). Serve warm alongside lime wedges, rice, flatbread or chickpea pancakes.

Photo on page 47.

CUMIN SQUASH STEW WITH CAULIFLOWER AND PINE NUT CRUMBLE

Serves 6

For the squash stew

500 g/1 lb 2 oz squash, cut in half and seeded

3 tablespoons extra-virgin olive oil, plus extra for drizzling

2 teaspoons cumin seeds

4 garlic cloves

Salt

2 onions, thinly sliced

225 g/8 oz (1 cup) brown lentils

1 tablespoon sumac

½ teaspoon ground cinnamon

1.5 litres/50 fl oz (6¼ cups) vegetable stock

Small bunch of mint, leaves only, chopped

Juice of 1 lime

For the cauliflower and pine nut crumble

1 small cauliflower (about 500 g/1 lb 2 oz)

4 tablespoons extra-virgin olive oil

Pinch of salt

50 g/1¾ oz (scant ½ cup) pine nuts

Small bunch of parsley, finely chopped

Photo on page 114.

Since preparing more veg-focused food, I've come to appreciate the importance of textures in a dish. Soupy or saucy dishes often benefit from an element of crunch in order to feel satisfied and excited by the food you're eating, and this stew is an embodiment of that principle. This stew is wonderfully hearty on its own, but the savoury crisp cauliflower and toasted pine nuts lift everything to delectable new heights. Generously drizzle olive oil over the finished stew to balance out the flavours.

Make the squash stew. Preheat the oven to 200°C/400°F/Gas Mark 6.

Using a peeler or knife, peel the squash. Place the flat side of the squash face down on the chopping (cutting) board. Cut the squash into 2-cm/¾-inch chunks, then spread out in a single layer on a roasting pan. Drizzle with oil to coat. Add the cumin seeds, 2 garlic cloves and a generous pinch of salt. Roast on the middle shelf for 25 minutes, until completely tender.

Meanwhile, heat the oil in a deep saucepan over medium heat, until it shimmers. Add the onions and ½ teaspoon of salt and sauté for 20 minutes, until the onions are caramelised.

Finely chop the remaining 2 garlic cloves, then add it to the pan and cook for another minute. Using a fork, roughly mash half of the roasted squash mixture and the roasted garlic cloves. Leave the other half chunky. Add the lentils, spices and all the squash to the pan. Pour in the stock, then bring to a boil. Cover, reduce the heat to medium-low and simmer for 25 minutes, until the lentils are completely tender. Remove the stew from the heat, then stir in the mint and lime juice. Keep warm over low heat.

Make the cauliflower and pine nut crumble. Thinly slice the cauliflower using a mandoline or knife.

Heat the oil in a large frying pan or skillet over high heat. Add the cauliflower and a pinch of salt and stir occasionally for 8–10 minutes, until the cauliflower is soft, nutty and charred in places. Stir in the pine nuts and cook for another minute. Stir in the parsley and remove from the heat.

Ladle the stew into warm bowls. Top with cauliflower crumble and a drizzle of extra-virgin olive oil.

RICE & GRAINS

L–R Lime and Herb Baked Rice (page 139), Lentil Soup with Tamarind and Greens (page 123).

BULGUR MUJADARA WITH NUTTY RED PEPPER SALSA

Serves 6 as a side

For the red pepper salsa

4 red Romano peppers

100 g/3½ oz (¾ cup) toasted walnuts, finely chopped

1 tablespoon Pomegranate Molasses (page 256)

1 garlic clove, crushed

½ teaspoon salt, plus extra

1 teaspoon Aleppo pepper

For the caramelised onions

4 tablespoons olive oil

3 red onions, thinly sliced

Pinch of salt

2 bay leaves

For the lentils

900 ml/30 fl oz (3¾ cups) vegetable stock

150 g/5½ oz (scant ¾ cup) brown lentils, rinsed

100 g/3½ oz (generous ½ cup) bulgur wheat

Bunch of chopped herbs, such as dill, parsley, mint and/or coriander (cilantro), to serve

In Syria, bulgur wheat is often used instead of rice. Traditionally, *mujadara* is served on its own as 'lentils and rice', but this version is bolstered by sweet roasted peppers. If you're short on time, use shop-bought roasted peppers – they're more acidic (courtesy of the vinegar), but they do the trick in a fix.

Make the red pepper salsa. Preheat the oven to 200°C/400°F/ Gas Mark 6. Line a baking sheet with parchment paper.

Place the peppers on the prepared baking sheet and roast for 45 minutes, turning every 15 minutes, until soft and charred in places. Transfer the peppers to a bowl, then quickly cover them with clingfilm (plastic wrap). Set aside for 30 minutes. (This will help to loosen the skins.)

Make the caramelised onions. Heat the oil in a large frying pan or skillet over medium heat for 1–2 minutes. Add the onions and salt and sauté for 6 minutes, until translucent. Reduce the heat to low, then add the bay leaves. Sauté for 30–40 minutes, until the onions are sweet and caramelised.

Meanwhile, make the lentils. Bring the stock to a boil in a medium saucepan. Add the lentils, then reduce the heat to medium-low. Cover and gently simmer for 15 minutes. Add the bulgur wheat in an even layer over the lentils and cover again. Simmer for another 10 minutes over medium heat. Take the pan off the heat, then cover and set aside for 15 minutes. (Do not peek!) Using a fork, gently fluff the lentils. Set aside.

Peel the pepper skins and remove the seeds. Discard both. Chop the peppers into ½-cm/¼-inch dice, then place them in a bowl. Add the remaining salsa ingredients and mix well. Season to taste with more salt. Set aside.

Add half of the caramelised onions to the lentil mixture. Transfer the mixture to a serving platter, then spoon over half of the red pepper salsa. Top with the remaining onions and herbs. Place the remaining salsa in a small bowl to serve alongside so everyone can help themselves.

Serve immediately.

Note

As part of a larger spread, I sometimes prepare triple the quantity of onions and double the lentil mixture for the Celebration Pie (page 191).

Photo includes Summer Vegetable Grain Salad on page 150.

NF

EGYPTIAN KOSHARI

Serves 6

1 tablespoon ghee

4 onions, thinly sliced

1 teaspoon salt, plus extra to taste

100 g/3½ oz (scant ½ cup) chickpeas, soaked overnight in ½ teaspoon salt and ½ teaspoon bicarbonate of soda

1 teaspoon bicarbonate of soda (baking soda)

6 tablespoons extra-virgin olive oil

250 g/9 oz (1 cup plus 3 tablespoons) basmati rice

4 garlic cloves, thinly sliced

2 fresh bay leaves

2 x (400-g/14-oz) cans chopped tomatoes

½ teaspoon chilli flakes

100 g/3½ oz dried vermicelli

1 teaspoon Baharat (page 254)

1 teaspoon ground cinnamon

1 teaspoon cumin seeds

250 g/9 oz (1¼ cups) cooked brown lentils

This dish requires a few pans for the various pulses (legumes) and grains, but many of the elements can be prepared in advance. In fact, the origin of this dish stems from using up leftovers, such as extra chickpeas from hummus.

In Cairo, most neighbourhoods have a favourite *koshari* joint, each one boasting their own recipe for the spiced tomato sauce. For me, this dish is all about the crispy onions and fried vermicelli, adding sweetness and crunch to every bite.

Heat the ghee in a large frying pan or skillet over medium-low heat. Add the onions and a pinch of the salt and sauté for 30–40 minutes, until the onions are sweet and caramelised. Transfer the onions to a paper towel–lined plate. Set aside.

Drain the soaked chickpeas, then place them in a saucepan. Cover with double the volume of cold water. Add the remaining salt and the bicarbonate of soda (baking soda) and bring to a boil over medium-high heat. Reduce the heat to medium-low and gently simmer for 30 minutes–1 hour, until the chickpeas are tender. Drain the chickpeas, then set aside.

Wipe out the saucepan. Heat 1 tablespoon of the oil over medium-high heat. Stir in the rice and mix until well coated. Toast for a minute. Pour in 475 ml/16 fl oz (2 cups) of water and cover. Boil for 2 minutes, then reduce the heat to low and cook for 5 minutes. Turn off the heat, cover and set aside for 10 minutes. (Do not peek!) Using a fork, fluff up the grains. Scrape the rice into a bowl, then set aside.

Wipe out the pan again. Heat 2 tablespoons of the oil over medium heat. Add the garlic and bay and sauté for a minute, until fragrant. Add the canned tomatoes. Fill a can with water and pour it into the mixture. Stir in the chilli and a pinch of salt. Simmer for 20 minutes, until the mixture is reduced by a third.

In a large frying pan or skillet, toast the vermicelli without any oil for 5 minutes over medium heat, until golden brown. Set aside.

Heat the remaining 3 tablespoons of oil in a saucepan over medium heat. Add the baharat, cinnamon and cumin and cook for a minute, until fragrant. Stir in the rice, lentils and chickpeas and cook for 5–7 minutes, until warmed through.

Transfer the *koshari* to a large serving platter or individual plates. Top with the tomato sauce, caramelised onions and crispy vermicelli.

The rice mixture, tomato sauce and onions can be stored separately in airtight containers in the refrigerator and the crispy vermicelli at room temperature for 3 days. Reheat to serve.

FREEKEH TABBOULEH

Serves 4

- 150 g/5½ oz (scant 1 cup) freekeh
- Salt and Aleppo pepper
- Large bunch of dill, leaves picked and chopped
- Large bunch of coriander (cilantro), leaves picked and chopped
- Large bunch of parsley, leaves picked and chopped
- Large bunch of mint, leaves picked and chopped
- Seeds from ½ pomegranate

Originating in the ancient Middle East, freekeh is a cracked wheat that turns smoky when charred. Traditional tabbouleh is often made with bulgur wheat with a 2:1 ratio of herbs to grain.

Cook the freekeh according to the package directions and add a pinch of salt to the cooking water. Drain the cooked freekeh, then transfer to a bowl. Stir in the herbs and mix well. Stir in the pomegranate seeds. Season to taste with salt and Aleppo pepper.

Transfer to a serving plate. The tabbouleh can be served slightly warm or at room temperature. Leftover tabbouleh can be covered and refrigerated for up to 3 days.

LIME AND HERB BAKED RICE

Serves 4 as a side

- 250 g/9 oz (1 cup plus 3 tablespoons) basmati rice
- 3 tablespoons extra-virgin olive oil
- 1 red onion, thinly sliced
- 2 fresh bay leaves
- 1½ teaspoons salt
- 1 mild red chilli
- Pared zest and juice of 1 unwaxed lime
- Bunch of herbs, such as dill, parsley, coriander (cilantro) and/or mint, chopped

Photo on page 132.

Baked rice is a fantastic way of imparting nuttiness and a crisp, toasted base for texture. The whole chilli flavours the rice without overpowering the dish with heat.

Be sure to choose unwaxed limes for this as you'll eat the skin. Unwaxed limes are processed with minimal chemical intervention.

Preheat the oven to 180°C/350°F/Gas Mark 4.

Place the rice in a fine-mesh sieve and rinse under cold running water for 3 minutes, until the water is clear. Transfer the rice to a bowl and cover with 3 times the volume of cold water.

Heat the oil in a casserole (Dutch oven) over medium heat. Add the onion, bay leaves and ½ teaspoon of the salt and sauté for 8 minutes until soft.

Meanwhile, cut the chilli in half lengthwise and scrape out the seeds, leaving the stalk intact. Add the chilli and drained rice to the pan and stir for a minute to briefly toast the rice. Add the pared lime zest to the pan.

Bring 475 ml/16 fl oz (2 cups) of water to a boil and add the remaining 1 teaspoon of salt. Pour over the rice. Cover with a lid or aluminium foil and bake for 30 minutes. Remove from the oven and keep covered for 5 minutes.

Discard the chilli, then fluff up the rice with a fork. Stir in the herbs and lime juice. Serve immediately.

OLIVE OIL BEANS WITH TOMATOES, GARLIC AND HERBS

Serves 4

2 x (400-g/14-oz) cans butter (lima) or cannellini beans, drained

150 ml/5 fl oz (⅔ cup) extra-virgin olive oil

4 garlic cloves, thinly sliced

2 teaspoons Aleppo pepper

1 teaspoon coriander seeds

1 Spiced Preserved Lime (page 260) or preserved lemon, flesh discarded and skin finely chopped

Handful of parsley, chopped

Handful of coriander (cilantro), chopped

2 tomatoes, grated

Salt and black pepper

Lebanese Flatbreads (page 198) and salty cheese, to serve

This simple dish is much greater than the sum of its parts, where the ingredients do most of the work during the 30-minute resting time. Grated tomatoes cut through the richness of the beans to add freshness.

Many of us keep olive oil for far too long, which can go rancid and bitter after opening. A good-quality olive oil tastes fresh and grassy and has a shelf life of about a year. If in doubt, invest in a new bottle of the good stuff.

Pat the beans dry with paper towels. Set aside.

Heat the oil in a small saucepan over medium heat for 2 minutes. Add the garlic, Aleppo pepper and coriander seeds and cook for 3–4 minutes, until the garlic sizzles and turns golden. Remove from the heat. Stir in the preserved lime or lemon, beans and herbs. Set aside for 30 minutes.

Transfer the beans to a serving bowl.

In a small bowl, combine the tomatoes and salt and pepper to taste, and mix well.

Top the beans with the tomatoes and serve immediately with flatbreads and salty cheese.

SYRIAN BLACK-EYED BEANS AND GREENS

Serves 4

200 g/7 oz (generous 1 cup) black-eyed beans (peas), drained

Salt and black pepper

1 teaspoon bicarbonate of soda (baking soda)

1 vegetable stock cube

200 g/7 oz spring greens or kale, tough stalks removed and leaves shredded

4 tablespoons extra-virgin olive oil

4 red onions, thinly sliced

1 tablespoon apple cider vinegar

150 g/5½ oz (scant 1 cup) couscous

215 ml/7¼ fl oz (scant 1 cup) hot vegetable stock

Small bunch of herbs, such as parsley, dill or coriander (cilantro), roughly chopped

1 lemon

***Sleek*, which should be made if only for its name, is a distant cousin of *Mujadara* (page 134) and *Koshari* (page 136). In this typical Syrian street food dish, grains and onions are the vehicle for spices and greens. All hardy greens work well here, so feel free to experiment with chard, kale and loose-leafed spring cabbage.**

In a large bowl, combine the beans, 1 teaspoon of salt and ½ teaspoon of bicarbonate of soda (baking soda). Add 3 times the volume in cold water and soak for 24 hours.

Drain the beans, then rinse in a colander under cold water. Transfer to a large saucepan and cover with 10 cm/4 inches of cold water. Bring the pan to a boil and crumble in the stock cube. Add the remaining ½ teaspoon of bicarbonate of soda (baking soda) and 1 tablespoon of salt. Reduce the heat to medium-low and simmer for 30 minutes. Add another 1 tablespoon of salt and cook for another 15–30 minutes, until the beans are completely tender. Stir in the greens and blanch for a minute. Drain in a colander, until all the steam has evaporated.

Meanwhile, heat the oil in a large frying pan or skillet over medium heat. Add the onions and 1 teaspoon of salt. Pour in the vinegar and sauté for 10 minutes, until the onions are soft and translucent. Reduce the heat to low and sauté for another 30 minutes, or until the onions are jammy and caramelised.

Pour the couscous into a heat-proof bowl and add the hot vegetable stock. Set aside for 5 minutes until all the liquid has been absorbed. Fluff up the grains with a fork.

Place a third of the onions onto a plate and set aside. Add the couscous, beans and greens to the pan and mix well. Season with salt and pepper.

Transfer to a platter. Top with the reserved onions and herbs. Grate the lemon zest over the platter, then squeeze over the lemon juice. Serve immediately.

POPPED BEANS WITH PICKLED RED ONION AND GARLIC LABNEH

Serves 4

For the garlic labneh

500 g/1 lb 2 oz (2¼ cups) Greek yogurt

Pinch of salt

2 garlic cloves, crushed

For the pickled red onion

1 small red onion, thinly sliced into rounds on a mandoline

1 tablespoon apple cider vinegar

½ teaspoon sugar

⅛ teaspoon salt

For the popped beans

1 x (600-g/1 lb 5-oz) jar butter (lima) beans or cannellini beans, drained

2 tablespoons extra-virgin olive oil, plus extra for drizzling

1 tablespoon sumac

1 teaspoon ground coriander

Small bunch of dill, to garnish

Lebanese Flatbreads (page 198), to serve

This dish is all about contrasts: cooling labneh is topped with hot crispy-on-the-outside, creamy-on-the-inside beans. (If you've never roasted beans, now is the time to start.) Sharp red onions are like jewels on top with an acidity that cuts through the richness of the dairy and beans.

I prefer jarred beans over their canned counterparts because they have a richer flavour and more pleasing texture. They're a bit pricier, but well worth it.

Make the garlic labneh. Line a colander with a piece of muslin (cheesecloth) and suspend the colander over a bowl. Add the yogurt, gather up the muslin sides to seal and drain the yogurt at room temperature for at least 3 hours or up to 12 for a firmer labneh. (The watery whey in the bowl can be used to make bread or replace filtered water when preserving vegetables.) Transfer the labneh to a mixing bowl.

Meanwhile, make the pickled red onion. In a small mixing bowl, combine all the ingredients and mix well. With clean hands, scrunch the mixture to work the sugar, salt and vinegar into the onion. (This softens their fiery flavour and turns them a beautiful shade of pink.) Place a clean jar or bowl on top of the onions to weigh them down and set aside for 1 hour to pickle. Alternatively, cover and refrigerate the pickle for up to 3 days.

Preheat the oven to 220°C/425°F/Gas Mark 7. Pat the beans dry with paper towels and spread out in a single layer on a baking sheet. Add the oil, sumac and ground coriander and toss to coat. Roast for 25 minutes, shaking the baking sheet twice during this time, so the beans brown and crisp evenly. Keep warm.

Sprinkle the salt over the garlic cloves. Chop and press down with the side of a knife continuously until a paste forms. Remove the labneh from the muslin, then transfer to a mixing bowl. Stir in the garlic.

Spread the labneh on a serving dish. Top with the popped beans and a handful of pickled onions. (Place the rest of the onion in a small dish to serve at the table.) Scatter over the dill and drizzle over more olive oil, which will pool in the labneh. Serve immediately with flatbreads.

QUICK FALAFEL

Serves 4

For the cucumber salad

2 tomatoes, roughly chopped
1 cucumber, roughly chopped
1 teaspoon sumac
Salt and black pepper

For the falafel

2 tablespoons olive oil
1 onion, finely chopped
Salt and black pepper
4 garlic cloves, minced
1 x (400-g/14-oz) can chickpeas, drained
Small bunch of parsley leaves, finely chopped, plus extra to garnish
35 g/1¼ oz (⅓ cup) gram flour
2 teaspoons ground cumin
1 teaspoon ground coriander
¼ teaspoon allspice
¼ teaspoon cayenne pepper
Juice from ½ lemon
Vegetable oil, for frying
4 pittas, toasted, to serve
Garlic Tahini Sauce (page 258), to serve

Traditionalists look away now. Classic falafel is made with dried chickpeas that have been soaked overnight, then blended into the mixture. Raising a family and working in the kitchen has taught me that you can't plan for every dinner. This fuss-free dish can be on the table in an hour, served with whatever you fancy.

Make the cucumber salad. Combine all the ingredients in a bowl and mix well.

Make the falafel. Heat the olive oil in a frying pan or skillet over medium heat, until it shimmers. Add the onion and a pinch of salt and sauté for 6–8 minutes, until soft and translucent. Add the garlic and sauté for a minute, until fragrant. Transfer the mixture to a bowl, then add all the remaining ingredients except the vegetable oil. Using a potato masher, crush the chickpeas until a rough paste forms. Chill in the refrigerator for 30 minutes.

Heat the vegetable oil in a deep frying pan or skillet to a depth of 3 cm/1¼ inches over medium-high heat. The oil is ready when a cube of bread dropped in sizzles on contact and turns golden in 20 seconds. (Alternatively, use a thermometer and heat to 180°C/350°F.)

With clean hands, shape the chilled falafel mixture into 40-g/1½-oz patties. Working in batches to avoid overcrowding, carefully lower 4 patties into the hot oil. Fry for 3 minutes, then flip with a slotted spoon and fry for another 3 minutes, until crisp and brown. Using the same slotted spoon, transfer the cooked falafel onto a paper towel–lined plate to drain. Repeat with the remaining falafel.

Sprinkle the falafel with parsley and serve with the cucumber salad, pittas and garlic tahini sauce.

PEA AND ZA'ATAR FALAFEL

Makes 18–20 falafel

200 g/7 oz (scant 1 cup) dried chickpeas, soaked with ½ teaspoon bicarbonate of soda (baking soda) for 24 hours

1 onion, roughly chopped

100 g/3½ oz (¾ cup) frozen peas, defrosted

2 tablespoons sesame seeds

2 teaspoons ground cumin

1 teaspoon ground coriander

1 teaspoon Za'atar (page 254)

½ teaspoon cayenne pepper

¼ teaspoon ground cardamom

½ teaspoon baking powder

2 teaspoons fine salt

Black pepper, to taste

Vegetable oil, for frying

To serve

Lebanese Flatbreads (page 198)

Arabic Garlic Sauce (page 258)

Chopped tomatoes

Chopped lettuce

Fermented Red Cabbage (page 63) or jarred pickled turnips (optional)

I always have a bag of peas in my freezer for quick pastas, sides and this recipe. Though green peas aren't traditional, I love the colour and sweetness they bring to these hot, crispy falafel, which will disappear as soon as they hit the table.

Serve these simply with flatbreads, tahini sauce and a chopped tomato salad or with herby grains and chopped cucumber.

Drain and rinse the chickpeas. In a food processor, combine all the ingredients, except for the vegetable oil, and pulse until well mixed. Transfer the mixture to a bowl, cover and chill in the refrigerator for at least 2 hours or overnight.

Heat the oil in a saucepan to a depth of 4 cm/1½ inches over medium heat. The oil is ready when a cube of bread dropped in sizzles on contact and turns golden in 30 seconds. (Alternatively, use a thermometer and heat to 160°C/325°F.) Shape the falafel mixture into balls, about 4 cm/1½ inches in diameter, or press slightly into patties. Working in batches, carefully lower them into the hot oil and fry for 2–3 minutes on each side, until golden and crispy. Using a slotted spoon, transfer the falafel to a paper towel–lined baking sheet to drain. Keep warm. Repeat with the remaining falafel.

Serve a few falafel with flatbreads, garlicky sauce, tomatoes, lettuce and pickled vegetables, if using.

SUMMER VEGETABLE GRAIN SALAD

Serves 4–6

- 200 g/7 oz (1 cup) freekeh
- Vegetable stock (optional)
- 100 g/3½ oz (¾ cup) fresh or frozen peas
- 10 radishes, quartered
- 2 bulbs fennel, thinly sliced
- Olive oil, for drizzling
- Salt and black pepper
- Grated zest and juice of 1 lemon
- Small bunch of spring onions (scallions), thinly sliced
- Small bunch of mixed herbs, such as basil, parsley, coriander (cilantro), dill and/or chervil, roughly chopped

Photo on page 135.

You could use any summer vegetable here, but the freshness of the suggested vegetables work well together. (Plus, the colour and textural contrasts are a feast for the eyes.)

I like to serve this alongside grilled halloumi and flatbreads for a more substantial meal.

Preheat the oven to 220°C/425°F/Gas Mark 7.

Cook the freekeh according to the package directions. Add a little vegetable stock to the cooking water for a richer flavour, if using. When the freekeh has a minute left of cooking, add the peas and cook for the final minute. Drain the freekeh and peas.

Combine the radishes and fennel in a large roasting pan and spread out in a single layer. If necessary, use 2 pans. Drizzle over enough olive oil to coat, then season well with salt and pepper. Roast for 25 minutes, until the vegetables have softened.

Scrape the hot vegetables into a large mixing bowl. Immediately, add the freekeh, peas and zest and juice of ½ lemon. Drizzle over a couple of glugs of olive oil. Toss in the spring onions (scallions) and herbs. Season to taste with salt, pepper and/or more lemon juice.

Serve at room temperature.

HERB AND COUSCOUS CAKE WITH PEPPER AND ALMOND SALSA

Serves 6

For the red pepper and almond salsa

2 large red peppers
2 tomatoes, cut in half
2 garlic cloves
50 g/1¾ oz (⅓ cup) toasted almonds
½ teaspoon salt
1 teaspoon hot smoked paprika
1½ teaspoons red wine vinegar
4 tablespoons extra-virgin olive oil
Honey or sugar, to sweeten
Salt and black pepper

For the couscous

200 g/7 oz (1 cup plus 2 tablespoons) couscous
1 teaspoon ground cumin
1 teaspoon ground coriander
½ teaspoon nigella seeds
½ teaspoon salt, plus extra
4 tablespoons extra-virgin olive oil
4 banana shallots, finely chopped
3 garlic cloves, finely chopped
30 g/1 oz parsley, stems finely chopped and leaves roughly chopped
30 g/1 oz coriander (cilantro), stems finely chopped and leaves roughly chopped
30 g/1 oz dill, stems finely chopped and leaves roughly chopped
75 g/2¾ oz (scant ¾ cup) pine nuts, toasted
2 eggs, beaten
75 g/2¾ oz crumbled feta
75 g/2¾ oz (⅔ cup) grated Parmesan-style cheese
150 g/5½ oz (scant ¾ cup) Greek yogurt
Black pepper
6 tablespoons light olive oil, for frying

Crumbly, nutty and full of flavour, this savoury cake tastes of sunshine. The smoky red pepper salsa is an amalgamation of two of my favourite sauces – *muhammara* from the Middle East and *romesco* from Spain. Both use a winning combination of red peppers and nuts in their most traditional forms.

One of the best things about this recipe is its adaptability. Replace the couscous with other cooked grains and the feta and Parmesan-style cheese with cheeses in the refrigerator that need using up.

Start the salsa. Preheat the oven to 200°C/400°F/Gas Mark 6.

Arrange the peppers and tomatoes, cut side up, on a baking sheet. Bake for 40 minutes, turning the peppers occasionally, until well charred and soft. Cover the baking sheet with aluminium foil, then set aside.

Make the couscous. In a heat-proof bowl, combine the couscous, spices and salt. Pour over 410 ml/14 fl oz (1⅔ cups) boiling water. Cover, then set aside for 5 minutes. Fluff up the couscous with a fork.

Heat 2 tablespoons of the extra-virgin olive oil in a large non-stick frying pan or skillet over medium heat. Add the shallots and a pinch of salt and sauté for 4–5 minutes, until soft and translucent. Add the garlic and herb stems and cook for another minute, until fragrant. Add the mixture to the bowl of couscous. Wipe the pan clean with paper towels to use again later. Stir in the herb leaves and pine nuts.

In a large bowl, combine the eggs, cheeses and yogurt and mix. Stir in the couscous mixture. Season generously with salt and pepper, then pour in the remaining 2 tablespoons of extra-virgin olive oil. Stir to combine.

Heat 3 tablespoons of the light olive oil in a non-stick frying pan over medium heat, until it shimmers. Using a serving spoon, transfer the couscous mixture to the pan. With the back of the spoon, press down on the couscous to compact it. Cook for 15 minutes, untouched, until the cake begins to turn golden and is set around the edge.

Recipe continued →

Recipe continued →

Meanwhile, make the rest of the salsa. Peel away the skins of the peppers, then remove the pith and seeds. Place the peppers and tomatoes in a food processor, then add the remaining salsa ingredients. Pulse until a chunky salsa forms. Season to taste with honey, salt and pepper. Transfer to a bowl and keep warm in a low oven.

To serve, place a large plate or board over the top of the pan. Using oven gloves (mitts) or a folded dish towel, hold both the pan and the plate with both hands. Quickly and confidently invert the cake onto the plate. Carefully lower the plate onto a work surface, then lift away the pan.

Heat the remaining 3 tablespoons of light olive oil over a medium heat. Shuffle the cake back to the pan, cooked side up. If it cracks, simply press it back together. Pan-fry for another 15 minutes to crisp the other side. Turn off the heat, then let the cake cool for 5 minutes in the pan.

Slice into 6 wedges, then serve with the salsa.

VEGETABLES

L–R Braised Cardamom Greens and Yogurt (page 160), Spiced Carrot Salad (page 74), Braised Runner Beans with Tomato and Cardamom (page 179).

GF

AUBERGINE AND TOMATO MEZZE

Serves 4

2 aubergines (eggplants)
3 tablespoons extra-virgin olive oil or ghee
1 onion, thinly sliced
½ teaspoon salt, plus extra
2 garlic cloves, thinly sliced
2 fresh bay leaves
1 x (400-g/14-oz) can cherry tomatoes
Pinch of sugar, plus extra
2 tablespoons pine nuts
2 tablespoons well-stirred tahini
2 sprigs dill, leaves picked

I used leftover pasta sauce to make this, embodying the spirit of Middle Eastern cuisine of wasting nothing and creating flavour-packed dishes from the simplest of ingredients. Use canned tomatoes or leftover tomato sauce if you have that.

The addition of aubergine (eggplant) rounds out this rich, buttery dip – and once you've made it, you'll see how deceptively simple it is.

Heat a griddle pan over high heat for at least 5 minutes. Add the aubergines (eggplants), turning every 3 minutes, until their skins are charred and the aubergines are collapsing. Set aside to cool.

Heat 2 tablespoons of the oil or ghee in a saucepan over medium heat. Add the onion and salt and sauté for 5 minutes, until the onion is translucent and soft. Reduce the heat to low and sauté for another 20–25 minutes, until the onion is jammy and caramelised. Increase the heat to medium. Add the garlic and bay leaves and cook for 3 minutes, until fragrant. Stir in the tomatoes, then bring to a boil. Cover, then reduce the heat to medium-low. Crush the tomatoes a few times to make a saucier mixture. Simmer for 15 minutes, stirring occasionally, until the sauce has reduced by a third. Season to taste with more salt and/or sugar. Set aside.

Heat the remaining tablespoon of oil or ghee in a frying pan or skillet over low heat. Add the pine nuts and sauté for 1½ minutes, until golden. Set aside.

When the aubergines are cool enough to handle, pull away the skins and the stalks and discard. Transfer the aubergine flesh to a mixing bowl. Using 2 forks, pull the flesh apart into ½-cm/¼-inch-wide strips of varying lengths. The aubergine should be completely soft and easy to work with.

Add the aubergine flesh to the pan and stir over medium-low heat, until warmed through. Drizzle over the tahini, then transfer the warm mixture to a serving plate. Top with the pine nuts and dill and serve immediately.

GF

BRAISED CARDAMOM GREENS AND YOGURT

Serves 4

2 dried black limes, roughly broken into pieces

2 tablespoons extra-virgin olive oil, plus extra for drizzling

1 onion, thinly sliced

Salt and black pepper

200 g/7 oz curly kale, finely shredded

Large bunch (about 100 g/3½ oz) parsley, stems finely chopped and leaves roughly chopped

Large bunch (about 100 g/3½ oz) dill, stems finely chopped and leaves roughly chopped

Large bunch (about 100 g/3½ oz) coriander (cilantro), stems finely chopped and leaves roughly chopped

Small bunch of spring onions (scallions) or 1 leek, white and light green parts only, thinly sliced

1 teaspoon dried mint

1 teaspoon ground cardamom

½ teaspoon ground cinnamon

250 g/9 oz (1 cup plus 2 tablespoons) Greek yogurt

1 tablespoon Za'atar (page 254)

This dish has its roots in Bahrain, where black lime is seemingly woven into every meal. If you've never cooked with it before, it's worth seeking out. Available from Middle Eastern and specialist online shops, it looks like a withered lump of charcoal and has a punchy, complex citrus flavour.

Flatbreads are perfect for mopping up the cooling yogurt and tender greens.

Place the black limes in a spice grinder and grind to a powder. Transfer to a bowl, then pour in 200 ml/7 fl oz (¾ cup plus 1 tablespoon) boiling water. Set aside.

Heat the olive oil in a deep frying pan or skillet over medium-low heat. Add the onion and a pinch of salt and sauté for 20 minutes, until caramelised. Stir in the kale, herb stems, spring onions (scallions), mint, cardamom and cinnamon.

Stir the black lime water to loosen any lime at the bottom of the bowl. Pour half of the liquid into the pan. Stir for 5 minutes, until the kale has wilted. Reduce the heat to low, then stir in the herb leaves and remaining lime water, including any remaining lime solids. Cook for 20 minutes, stirring occasionally, until the greens have completely softened.

Meanwhile, combine the yogurt, a generous pinch of salt and a grind of black pepper in a bowl.

Spread the seasoned yogurt on a platter and sprinkle over the za'atar. Drizzle over 2 tablespoons of olive oil. Top with the greens and season well with salt and pepper. Drizzle over another tablespoon of olive oil and serve immediately.

CHARRED SUMMER CABBAGE WITH POMEGRANATE MOLASSES AND WALNUTS

Serves 6

- 3 tablespoons walnuts
- ½ teaspoon cumin seeds
- 1 tablespoon olive oil
- 500 g/1 lb 2 oz pointed or hispi cabbage, outer leaves removed, cored and finely shredded
- Pinch of salt
- 1 tablespoon Pomegranate Molasses (page 256)
- Lebanese Flatbreads (page 198), toasted, to serve
- Greek yogurt, to serve

Pictured opposite.

I cook this dish again and again throughout the year, probably owing to its simplicity. It's an explosion of delicious flavours from a few ingredients that you're likely to have in the cupboard. In the winter, I sometimes make this with finely shredded Brussels sprouts, which require a little more time in the pan.

Toast the walnuts in a dry frying pan or skillet over low heat for 6–8 minutes, shaking the pan frequently, until golden and toasted. Add the cumin seeds and toast for 30 seconds, until fragrant. Transfer to a plate and set aside until later.

Heat the oil in the same pan over medium-high heat. Add the cabbage and salt. Sauté for 5 minutes, until the leaves have started to reduce in size. (You still want them to be a vibrant green.) Stir in the pomegranate molasses, walnuts and cumin. Cook for another 30 seconds, tossing the pan a couple of times until everything is incorporated.

Serve warm alongside toasted flatbread and yogurt.

GRILLED CORN ON THE COB WITH SUMAC BUTTER

Serves 4 as a side

- 1 teaspoon fine salt
- 2 ears of corn
- 3½ tablespoons butter
- 1 mild green chilli, finely chopped
- 2 teaspoons sumac
- Flaky sea salt, to finish

Hot, spiced sweetcorn is sold from street carts across the Middle East. It's sold in paper wrappers as a quick, on-the-go snack and served with different accompaniments, depending on your location in the Levant: from punchy, vibrant zhug to za'atar. I love sumac's sharp, lemony contrast to the sweet kernels.

Be generous with the salt when the corn is hot off the grill (broiler).

Bring a large saucepan of water to a boil. Add the salt and corn. Boil for 5 minutes. Drain, then pat dry with paper towels.

Preheat a griddle pan over high heat for 5 minutes.

Meanwhile, melt the butter in a frying pan or skillet, until it foams. Add the chilli and sumac. Add the corn and brush all over with the sumac butter. Turn every 2 minutes, brushing with more butter, until the corn is charred in places and smoky all over.

Slice the corn cobs in half, then transfer to a warm serving plate. Drizzle over any remaining sumac butter and sprinkle over a pinch of flaky sea salt. Serve.

BEETROOT AND FETA FRITTERS WITH CUMIN-DILL YOGURT

Serves 4

For the fritters

3 tablespoons neutral oil

1 onion, finely chopped

Salt and black pepper

300 g/10½ oz beetroot (beet), peeled and grated

75 g/2¾ oz crumbled feta

¼ teaspoon ground coriander

¼ teaspoon dried mint

Pinch of chilli flakes

90 g/3¼ oz (generous ½ cup) plain (all-purpose) flour

½ teaspoon bicarbonate of soda (baking soda)

150 ml/5 fl oz (⅔ cup) milk

1 lemon, cut into wedges

Flaky sea salt, to serve

Tomato and Pomegranate Salad (page 74), to serve (optional)

For the yogurt

150 ml/5 fl oz (⅔ cup) Greek yogurt

½ teaspoon cumin seeds, toasted

½ small bunch of dill, leaves only

Grated zest of 1 lemon

Black pepper

Here's something I'd be happy to serve and eat at any time of day – plus, they have the bonus of being simple to prepare. Enjoy them with a fried egg in the morning, alongside a chopped salad for lunch or as part of a mezze feast. The creamy yogurt sauce – seasoned with cumin, lemon and pepper – balances out the flavours.

Make the fritters. Heat 1 tablespoon of the oil in a frying pan or skillet over medium-low heat. Add the onion and a pinch of salt and sauté for 6–8 minutes, until soft and translucent.

In a bowl, combine the beetroot (beet), feta and spices.

In a separate bowl, combine the flour, bicarbonate of soda (baking soda) and milk and whisk until smooth. Add the beetroot mixture and stir until combined. Season generously with salt and pepper. Chill in the refrigerator for 15 minutes.

Heat the remaining 2 tablespoons of oil in a large frying pan or skillet over medium-high heat. Place a spoonful of the chilled batter into the hot oil, which should sizzle as soon as it hits the pan. Working in batches to avoid overcrowding, fry for 3 minutes on each side until golden and crisp. Transfer the cooked fritters to a paper towel-lined plate. Keep warm in a low oven while you cook the rest.

Make the yogurt. Combine all the ingredients in a bowl and mix well. Season to taste with pepper. It should be warming but not overpowering.

Serve the warm fritters with the yogurt, a wedge of lemon and pinch of flaky sea salt. Alternatively, for a more substantial meal, serve them alongside the salad.

CAULIFLOWER MUSAKHAN

Serves 4

For the spice mix

½ teaspoon grated nutmeg
2 tablespoons sumac
1 teaspoon ground cinnamon
½ teaspoon ground allspice
¼ teaspoon ground cardamom
¼ teaspoon salt

For the cauliflower

1 large cauliflower (about 1 kg/2 lb 4 oz), leaves separated and reserved
4 tablespoons ghee
100 ml/3½ fl oz (scant ½ cup) Greek yogurt
3 white onions, cut into 1-cm/½-inch slices
Salt
3 sprigs parsley, chopped

To serve

½ quantity Taboon Bread (page 209) or Lebanese Flatbreads (page 198)
Greek yogurt
3 tablespoons Fermented Red Cabbage (page 63) (optional)

Musakhan **is a Palestinian dish more often made with chicken thighs, but this cauliflower version, which uses both the leaves and florets, is a firm favourite. Adorned with pine nuts, this dish is for times of celebration and symbolises prosperity ahead.**

I usually serve this with Taboon Bread (page 209) and pickles, but I'm sure it would be lovely alongside cooked grains.

Preheat the oven to 200°C/400°F/Gas Mark 6.

Make the spice mix. Combine all the ingredients in a small bowl and mix well.

Make the cauliflower. Cut the cauliflower into 2-cm/¾-inch florets. Place in a bowl. Cut the leaves into 1-cm/½-inch cubes, discarding the tough core. Place them in a separate bowl. Set aside.

Melt 2 tablespoons of the ghee in a microwave or saucepan. Pour the melted ghee and yogurt over the cauliflower florets. Sprinkle in half of the spice mixture and toss to coat. Set aside to marinate.

Melt the remaining 2 tablespoons of ghee in a large ovenproof frying pan or skillet over medium heat. Add the onions and a large pinch of salt and sauté for 20 minutes, until soft, jammy and caramelised. Add the remaining spice mix and sauté for another minute, until fragrant. Nestle the marinated cauliflower florets into the onions and roast for 35 minutes. (Alternatively, transfer the onions to a large roasting dish and nestle the cauliflower florets on top.)

Meanwhile, bring a large saucepan of water to a boil. Add the cauliflower leaves and blanch for 4 minutes. Drain, then set aside to cool. When cool enough to handle, finely shred the leaves, leaving any smaller leaves whole.

When the florets have finished roasting, scatter the leaves on top. Roast for another 8 minutes, until crispy in places. Scatter over the parsley.

Serve the musakhan with a bread, yogurt and fermented red cabbage, if using.

DUKKAH-CRUSTED HALLOUMI SKEWERS

Makes 8 skewers

For the marinade

2 garlic cloves, crushed

2 teaspoons dried mint

½ teaspoon salt

5 tablespoons extra-virgin olive oil

1 tablespoon red wine vinegar

1 teaspoon date syrup

Grated zest and juice of 1 lemon

For the kebabs

1 red onion, halved lengthwise from tip to root

2 red Romano peppers, seeded and sliced into 8 strips

1 aubergine (eggplant), cut into 2-cm/¾-inch triangles

250 g/9 oz halloumi, soaked in cold water for 1 hour and patted dry with paper towels

5 tablespoons Dukkah (page 255)

Extra-virgin olive oil, for brushing

Lebanese Flatbreads (page 198), to serve

Chopped salad, to serve

Dukkah is an aromatic blend of spices, nuts and seeds that's often served as a dip with olive oil and bread. Here, it acts as a crunchy, flavourful coating for vegetable and halloumi kebabs.

I provide a recipe for homemade dukkah (page 255), but it's generally available in the spice section of large supermarkets. Be sure to pre-soak the halloumi, which removes some of the saltiness but also prevents the cheese from turning rubbery and burning during cooking.

Soak 8 bamboo skewers in cold water for 1 hour.

Meanwhile, make the marinade. In a large bowl, combine all the ingredients and mix well. Set aside.

Make the kebabs. Cut the onion into quarters through the root. (This helps to hold the layers of onion together.) Put the onion, peppers and aubergine (eggplant) into the bowl with the marinade.

Cut the halloumi into 24 × 2-cm/ ¾-inch cubes and add to the bowl. With clean hands, toss well to coat everything in the marinade. Set aside for 1 hour. This ensures that the vegetables are richly flavoured throughout and begin to soften before they cook.

Preheat the grill (broiler) to a high heat. Line a baking sheet with aluminium foil.

Thread the vegetables and cheese alternately onto the soaked skewers. Place on the prepared baking sheet, then discard any remaining marinade. (Any remaining vegetables can be grilled to toss through rice or grains.) Grill the skewers for 12 minutes, turning every 3 minutes, until the vegetables are soft and beginning to char.

Meanwhile, spread the dukkah on a plate.

Remove the kebabs from the heat, then immediately brush each with olive oil to coat. Turn the skewers in the dukkah, until well coated.

Serve with flatbreads and a simple chopped salad.

GOLDEN PUMPKIN WITH SAFFRON-BUTTER SAUCE

Serves 4 as a main with bread or rice, or 6 as a side

For the pumpkin

1 kg/2 lb 4 oz pumpkin, seeded and cut into 1-cm/½-inch crescents

Olive oil, to coat

1 teaspoon chilli flakes

1 teaspoon ground cinnamon

1 teaspoon salt

For the saffron-butter sauce

Pinch of saffron strands, soaked in 1 tablespoon boiling water

1 tablespoon white wine vinegar

60 g/2¼ oz cold butter, cut into 1-cm/½-inch cubes

To serve

400 g/14 oz (1⅔ cups) Greek yogurt

4 tablespoons Dukkah (page 255)

Gold on gold: this tender pumpkin dish is the most luxurious thing I've tasted in a while. The thick and unctuous saffron-butter sauce is delicious over the sweet pumpkin, but it would be lovely with most vegetables.

The mild acidity from the yogurt balances out the richness of the dish. Serve it with a dressed green salad and flatbreads for a majestic dinner.

Make the pumpkin. Preheat the oven to 220°C/425°F/Gas Mark 7.

Place the pumpkin in a large baking dish. Drizzle over enough oil to coat, then toss until well-coated. Add the spices and salt and toss again. Roast for 25–30 minutes, until the pumpkin is very tender and can be easily pierced with a knife without any resistance.

Meanwhile, make the saffron-butter sauce. Add the saffron and its soaking liquid along with the vinegar to a small saucepan. Pour in 100 ml/3½ fl oz (scant ½ cup) water, then bring to a boil. Boil for 5 minutes, or until it has reduced by half. Remove from the heat.

Whisk in the butter cubes, one by one, only adding more after each addition has melted. Once all the butter has been incorporated, the sauce should be thick, emulsified and vibrant, like the colour of bright egg yolk.

Spread the yogurt on a serving platter, top with the pumpkin and drizzle over the sauce. Scatter over half the dukkah, then place the remainder in a small bowl. (Guests can add more crunch to their pumpkin at the table.) Serve immediately.

GF

SPINACH BORANI WITH WALNUTS

Serves 4 as a starter

2 tablespoons olive oil or ghee
1 onion, thinly sliced
Pinch of salt, plus extra
300 g/10½ oz spinach, well rinsed
1 garlic clove, thinly sliced
200 g/7 oz (scant 1 cup) Greek yogurt
Juice of ½ lemon, plus extra
4 walnut halves
Extra-virgin olive oil, for drizzling
Lebanese Flatbreads (page 198) or crudités, to serve

A popular Persian invention, *boranis* are usually a combination of thick yogurt and spinach or beetroot (beets). The caramelised onions work particularly well in this recipe – the sweetness of the onion cuts through the sharp creaminess of the yogurt so everything is perfectly balanced.

It's also incredibly healthy. There's enough spinach in this borani to make Popeye a fan.

Heat 1 tablespoon of the oil or ghee in a small frying pan or skillet over medium heat. Add the onion and salt and sauté for 6–8 minutes, until completely soft. Reduce the heat to medium-low and sauté for another 20 minutes, until the onion turns dark golden and jammy. Transfer the onion to a plate, then set aside.

Add the spinach to a large frying pan or skillet and cook over medium heat, until wilted. (The water clinging to the leaves after they've been washed will help with this.) Transfer the wilted spinach to a colander and set aside to drain. When cool enough to handle, squeeze as much water from the spinach as you can and finely chop.

Heat the remaining tablespoon of oil over medium heat. Add the garlic and sauté for a minute, until it just begins to colour. Stir in the spinach and cook for another minute. Transfer to a mixing bowl. Stir in the yogurt and lemon juice. Season to taste with more salt or lemon juice, if needed.

Transfer the spinach borani to a serving bowl. Top with the caramelised onions, walnuts and a drizzle of extra-virgin olive oil. Serve with flatbreads or crudités.

TOMATO AND MINT MEZZE

Serves 4

2 tablespoons extra-virgin olive oil
1 onion, thinly sliced
Pinch of salt, plus extra
1 kg/2 lb 4 oz vine tomatoes
2 fresh bay leaves
2 garlic cloves, finely chopped
1 cinnamon stick
1 teaspoon dried mint

To serve
1 tablespoon ghee
6 garlic cloves, thinly sliced
2 tablespoons flaked (slivered) almonds
Extra-virgin olive oil, for drizzling
4 sprigs dill, leaves only
Lebanese Flatbread (page 198) or crackers

Photo on page 96.

Known in Arabic as *galayet bandoura*, this dish has its roots in Jordan, where tomatoes grow plentifully. Because it's so easy to prepare, it's a popular dish on camping and hiking trips, cooked over a simple wooden fire.

It is best with Arabic flatbreads and pickles. It's also delicious alongside grain salads, pan-fried tofu, or grilled aubergines (eggplants) and feta.

Heat the oil in a large frying pan or skillet over medium heat, until it shimmers. Add the onion and a pinch of salt. Fry for 5 minutes, stirring regularly, until the onion turns translucent. Turn the heat down to low and cook for 15 minutes, stirring occasionally, until the onion is caramelised.

Meanwhile, use a serrated knife to make a cross in the base of each tomato, just to pierce the skin. Bring a large saucepan of salted water to a boil. Lower the tomatoes into the pan and cook for 2 minutes. Using a slotted spoon, transfer the tomatoes to a chopping (cutting) board to cool. When the tomatoes are still warm but cool enough to handle, peel away the skins and discard. Chop the tomatoes into 8 wedges. Set aside.

Add the bay leaves and garlic to the frying pan and sauté for a minute, until fragrant. Stir in the tomatoes. Add the cinnamon and mint. Reduce the heat to low and simmer for 25–30 minutes, until there is no juice left in the pan and the tomatoes begin to caramelise.

Heat the ghee in a small frying pan or skillet over medium heat. Add the garlic and almonds and sauté for 2–3 minutes until golden.

Discard the cinnamon stick and bay leaves from the tomato mixture. Spoon the tomato into a serving bowl and top with the garlic and almonds. Drizzle over more olive oil and top with the dill. Serve with flatbreads or crackers.

The tomato mixture can be covered and stored in the refrigerator for up to 3 days.

HARISSA AND LIME AUBERGINES WITH CRUSHED CHICKPEAS

Serves 4

For the aubergines (eggplants) and chickpeas

2 large aubergines (eggplants), cut lengthwise into 5-mm/¼-inch slices

Extra-virgin olive oil, for drizzling

Salt and black pepper

1 x (600-g/1 lb 5-oz) can chickpeas, drained

1 garlic clove

1 tablespoon Rose Harissa (page 256)

Juice of 1 lime, plus extra

Lebanese Flatbreads (page 198), warmed, to serve

For the herby yogurt

6 tablespoons Greek yogurt

½ small bunch coriander (cilantro), leaves only, chopped

½ small bunch mint, leaves only, chopped

½ small bunch dill, leaves only, chopped

Juice of ½ lime

For the garnish

Seeds from ½ pomegranate

Handful of coriander (cilantro) leaves, roughly chopped

Handful of mint leaves, roughly chopped

Handful of dill, leaves picked

½ bunch spring onions (scallions), sliced diagonally

2 tablespoons toasted pumpkin seeds

Smoky grilled aubergines (eggplants) always evoke the smells of hectic street food stalls in my homeland. You could barbecue aubergines instead – just be sure to oil the slices first (opposed to what I've instructed here), which prevents your kitchen becoming too smoky.

Make the aubergines (eggplants) and chickpeas. Warm a griddle pan over the highest heat for 5 minutes.

Working in batches, add the aubergine (eggplant) slices to the pan and grill them for 3 minutes on each side, until char marks form. Resist the temptation of moving them around too much. Transfer to a roasting pan, then drizzle with the oil and season with salt and pepper. Repeat until all the aubergine slices are cooked.

Preheat an oven to 200°C/400°F/Gas Mark 6. Spread out the aubergines in a single layer across 1–2 roasting pans. Roast for 5 minutes, then turn off the oven and keep the aubergine warm in the residual heat with the door closed.

Pulse the chickpeas in a food processor a few times, until roughly chopped. Add the garlic, harissa, lime juice, salt and pepper and pulse again. Season to taste with salt, pepper and/or lime juice.

Make the herby yogurt. Combine all the ingredients and mix well. Chill for 30 minutes.

Arrange the crushed chickpeas on a platter, then lay the aubergine slices on top. Drizzle over half the yogurt mixture. Transfer the rest of the mixture to a bowl for guests to help themselves when at the table. Sprinkle over the pomegranate seeds, herbs, spring onions (scallions) and toasted seeds.

Serve with warm flatbreads.

LEMON AND HONEY POTATOES

Serves 4 as a side

1.25 kg/2 lb 6 oz floury (baking) potatoes, such as Maris Piper, cut into 2-cm/¾-inch wedges
100 ml/3½ fl oz (scant ½ cup) olive oil
2 tablespoons semolina (farina)
1 teaspoon dried thyme
Juice of 1 lemon
½ teaspoon salt, plus extra
Black pepper
3 tablespoons honey

Having lived in the UK since the 1960s, I've developed a passion for the humble spud in all its forms. This roasted version, though, has its roots firmly in the Middle East, with aromatic thyme lending a sweet, woody character to the crispy, caramelised potatoes.

Don't be put off by the amount of oil required to cook the potatoes – it keeps them tender and prevents them from burning while they cook.

Place the potatoes in a large bowl of cold water and set aside for 45 minutes. This helps to draw out starch from the potatoes, so that they can crisp up in the oven.

Preheat the oven to 220°C/425°F/Gas Mark 7.

Meanwhile, in a large bowl, combine the oil, semolina (farina), thyme, lemon juice, salt and 3 tablespoons water.

Using a slotted spoon, transfer the potatoes to the bowl. (Do not drain them in a colander, as this washes the starch back over the potatoes.) Toss the potatoes to coat, then spread them out in a single layer over 2 baking sheets. Divide any remaining liquid between the 2 sheets. Season well with salt and pepper.

Roast the potatoes for 40 minutes, turning halfway, and opening the oven 2 or 3 times to release the steam. Drizzle the honey over the potatoes, then roast for another 10 minutes, until glossy and golden.

Serve immediately.

Photo includes Baked Spicy Potatoes on page 178.

BAKED SPICY POTATOES

Serves 6 as a side

1 kg/2 lb 4 oz floury (baking) potatoes, cut into 2-cm/¾-inch cubes

4 tablespoons extra-virgin olive oil

1 tablespoon coriander seeds

1 teaspoon ground cumin

1 teaspoon ground turmeric

1 teaspoon Aleppo pepper

1 lemon, cut in half

Salt and black pepper

Small bunch of parsley, leaves only, roughly chopped

Photo on page 177.

I'd bet a princely sum on the fact that a version of this dish is on the menu of most Lebanese restaurants around the world. Known as *batata harra* ('spicy potatoes'), this dish is most often fried or deep-fried, but this roasted version suits me better. Pre-soaking the potatoes removes the starch, helping the potatoes crisp up in the oven. And since the oven does all the hard work, I'm not chained to the stove and free to put my feet up.

Place the potatoes in a large mixing bowl and cover with double the volume of cold water. Set aside for 1 hour. (Don't be tempted to skip this step – this will draw out the starch from the potatoes and help them to crisp up in the oven.)

Preheat the oven to 220°C/425°F/Gas Mark 7.

Using a slotted spoon, transfer the potatoes to a clean, empty bowl. (Do not drain them in a colander, as this washes the starch back over the potatoes.) Pat dry with paper towels.

Pour the oil into a large roasting pan and place on the middle shelf in the oven for 3 minutes to heat. Carefully remove the tray with the hot oil from the oven, then carefully spread the potatoes in an even layer (they will sizzle). Add the spices and use a rubber spatula to mix everything together. Bake for 15 minutes. Turn the potatoes over with the spatula. Nestle the lemon halves among the potatoes. Bake for another 30 minutes, turning the potatoes every 10 minutes or so, until crisp and golden. Season well with salt and pepper.

Discard the lemon halves. Sprinkle with parsley, then transfer the potatoes to a warm serving dish. Serve immediately.

BRAISED RUNNER BEANS WITH TOMATO AND CARDAMOM

Serves 4 as a side

6 tablespoons extra-virgin olive oil, plus extra for drizzling
1 onion, thinly sliced
½ teaspoon salt
6 garlic cloves, thinly sliced
3 fresh bay leaves
6 cardamom pods, crushed
½ teaspoon Aleppo pepper
4 tomatoes, roughly chopped
400 g/14 oz runner beans, ends trimmed and sliced diagonally into 1-cm/½-inch pieces
1 teaspoon red wine vinegar
Black pepper
2 sprigs dill, leaves only
Rice or Lebanese Flatbread (page 198), to serve (optional)

Photo on page 157.

While slow-braising perky summer vegetables like green beans may seem counter-intuitive, I much prefer eating them this way – they turn almost silky over an extended cooking time and absorb so much flavour.

Dill adds a grassy, aniseed element but other fresh herbs such as parsley or chives will work well, too. The addition of tangy feta or a dollop of yogurt adds a deliciously rich creaminess to the tender beans. No matter how you serve it, be generous with the olive oil.

Heat the oil in a saucepan over medium heat, until it shimmers. Add the onion and ½ teaspoon of salt and sauté for 8–10 minutes, until the onion is translucent. Stir in the garlic, bay leaves, cardamom and Aleppo pepper and cook for another minute, until fragrant.

Stir in the tomatoes and a pinch of salt and sauté for 10 minutes, until the tomatoes are soft.

Add the beans, then bring the mixture to a simmer. Cover, reduce the heat to low and cook for 60 minutes, stirring occasionally.

Stir in the vinegar, then cover and cook for another 30 minutes, until the beans are silky and completely soft. Season to taste with salt and pepper.

Spoon the beans into a serving bowl, then top with the dill and drizzle with olive oil. Serve on its own or with rice or flatbread for a more substantial meal.

The beans can be covered and stored in the refrigerator for 3 days. (They often taste better the next day.)

ROASTED CARROT MEZZE

Serves 4

500 g/1 lb 2 oz carrots, cut into irregular 2-cm/¾-inch pieces
1 cinnamon stick
2 teaspoons coriander seeds
½ teaspoon salt
Juice of 1 lemon
1 garlic clove
½ thumb-sized piece of fresh ginger, grated
4 tablespoons extra-virgin olive oil
2 tablespoons pine nuts
1 teaspoon cumin seeds
Greek yogurt, to garnish (optional)
Coriander (cilantro) leaves, to garnish
Lebanese Flatbreads (page 198), warmed, to serve

Roasting carrots intensifies and caramelises their sweet, earthy flavour, which just so happens to work well with the spices and citrus in this mezze. Any extra mezze will keep covered in the refrigerator for up to three days and can be spread in a sandwich with pickles, ricotta or grilled halloumi for a quick and satisfying lunch.

Preheat the oven to 160°C/325°F/Gas Mark 3.

In a roasting pan, combine the carrots, cinnamon stick, coriander seeds, salt and lemon juice. Add 200 ml/7 fl oz (¾ cup plus 1 tablespoon) of water and cover the dish with aluminium foil. Bake for 1½ hours, until the carrots can be easily pierced with a knife without any resistance.

Transfer half of the carrots to a food processor. Add the garlic, ginger and 1 tablespoon of water and process until smooth.

Transfer the remaining carrots to a bowl. Using a fork, mash the carrots to a slightly chunky texture. Mix in the carrot purée. Arrange on a platter.

Heat the oil in a small frying pan or skillet over medium heat. Add the pine nuts and toast for 3 minutes, until golden. Remove from the heat, then immediately stir in the cumin seeds, which should sizzle immediately. Pour this mixture over the carrots, then top with a dollop of yogurt, if using. Garnish with coriander (cilantro) leaves.

Serve warm or at room temperature with hot flatbreads.

ROASTED COURGETTE SALAD WITH HALLOUMI AND MINT

Serves 4

- 2 courgettes (zucchini), sliced diagonally into 1-cm/½-inch rounds
- Extra-virgin olive oil, for drizzling
- Pinch of salt
- 225 g/8 oz halloumi, cut into 2-cm/¾-inch cubes and soaked in cold water for 1 hour
- Handful of mint leaves
- 1 teaspoon dried mint
- 35 g/1¼ oz black olives, pitted and roughly chopped
- Grated zest and juice of ½ lemon

I often make this fresh salad for lunch as it can be on the table in 25 minutes, and it keeps well until the following day. Pre-soak the halloumi to ensure it stays tender and doesn't burn when cooking.

For a more substantial meal, serve it with rice or freekeh.

Preheat the oven to 170°C/340°F/Gas Mark 3. Line a baking sheet with parchment paper.

Place the courgettes (zucchini) on the prepared baking sheet in an even layer. Drizzle with oil and add a pinch of salt. Toss to coat, then spread out into a single layer. Roast for 20–25 minutes, until soft and caramelised in places.

Drain the halloumi, then pat dry with paper towels. Heat a large, non-stick frying pan or skillet over medium heat. Add the halloumi and pan-fry without oil for 8 minutes, until golden. Remove from the heat.

Transfer the courgettes to a serving platter. Toss gently with the halloumi, fresh and dried mint, olives and lemon zest and juice. Drizzle with oil. Serve warm or at room temperature.

SAVOURY BAKLAVA PIE

Serves 4

3 tablespoons extra-virgin olive oil
1 onion, finely chopped
½ teaspoon salt, plus extra
Black pepper
3 garlic cloves, minced
1 green chilli, finely chopped
200 g/7 oz kale or spring greens, finely chopped
1 teaspoon ground coriander
150 g/5½ oz crumbled feta
75 g/2¾ oz (⅔ cup) toasted walnuts, roughly chopped
Small bunch of chives, finely chopped
Small bunch of parsley, finely chopped
Small bunch of dill, finely chopped
2 eggs, beaten
3 tablespoons melted ghee or butter, plus extra for brushing
9 sheets filo (phyllo) pastry
2 tablespoons sesame seeds
Your favourite pickle, to serve
Lemon and Honey Potatoes (page 176), to serve

This flaky filo (phyllo) pie takes its inspiration from Greek spanakopita, the iconic savoury pie dish that's ideal for picnics, parties and plush lunches with friends.

I've given my pie a few extra adornments. And unlike spanakopita, which brushes the top layer of filo with olive oil, I prefer brushing ghee over each filo layer for crisp results.

A food processor chops vegetables quickly and evenly, but if you're so inclined, prepping the onions, greens and herbs separately by hand can be a meditative way to spend 20 minutes.

Preheat the oven to 180°C/350°F/Gas Mark 4.

Heat the oil in a deep frying pan or skillet over medium heat. Add the onion and the salt and sauté for 10 minutes, until soft and translucent. Stir in the garlic, chilli and greens and sauté, for 30 seconds. Cover and steam for 5 minutes, checking occasionally to ensure that the greens aren't sticking and taking on any colour. If so, turn the heat down to continue to cook the greens gently.

Stir in the coriander, then remove the pan from the heat.

Transfer the mixture into a large bowl. Stir in the feta, walnuts and herbs. Season to taste with salt and pepper. Mix in the eggs and set aside.

Brush the bottom and sides of a rimmed 20 × 30-cm/8 × 12-inch baking dish with melted ghee or butter. Lay a sheet of filo (phyllo) over the bottom, folding in any of the pastry that is wider than the dish. Brush all over with the melted ghee. Repeat with 2 more filo sheets. Spread out half of the greens over the pastry, covering as much of the filo as possible. Lay another sheet of filo on top, then brush with ghee. Repeat again with 2 more sheets. Finish layering the pie with the remaining greens and 3 layers of pastry. Score the pie into 12 large diamonds and sprinkle sesame seeds over the centre of each shape. Bake for 45 minutes, until golden on top. Set aside for 5 minutes.

Serve warm with pickles and lemon and honey potatoes.

WHITE BEAN PKAILA WITH HARISSA SQUASH

- 800 g/1 lb 12 oz spinach
- Bunch of parsley
- Bunch of coriander (cilantro)
- 1 onion, roughly chopped
- 150 ml/5 fl oz (⅔ cup) extra-virgin olive oil, plus extra for drizzling and greasing
- 4 garlic cloves, thinly sliced
- 1 small (800 g/1 lb 12 oz) pumpkin, seeded and cut into 3-cm/1¼-inch-thick crescents
- 1 teaspoon ground cumin
- 1 teaspoon Aleppo pepper
- ½ teaspoon ground cinnamon
- 1½ teaspoons salt, plus extra
- 1 tablespoon Rose Harissa (page 256)
- 1 Spiced Preserved Lime (page 260), rinsed
- ½ teaspoon ground cardamom
- 800 g/1 lb 12 oz cooked or canned white beans
- Grated zest and juice of 2 lemons
- Black pepper
- Lebanese Flatbreads (page 198), warmed, or rice, to serve (optional)

A wonderfully indulgent way to eat more greens, *pkaila* is a Tunisian-Jewish technique whereby dark green leaves, such as spinach or Swiss chard, are cooked down for hours in generous quantities of olive oil to create a super-concentrated spinach paste that turns almost black. As the flavour is so potent, it can also be used as a condiment to flavour bean soups and stews.

Working in batches, combine the spinach, herbs and onion in a food processor and finely chop. (Depending on the capacity of your food processor, this may need to be done in several batches – anywhere from 4–8 is normal. Alternatively, chop everything by hand, but this will take considerably more time.)

Transfer the chopped ingredients to a large saucepan. Sauté over medium heat for 10 minutes, until little liquid is left but before the spinach begins to catch on the base. Stir in the olive oil and garlic and cook for another 5 minutes, until fragrant. Reduce the heat to low and cook for 2–2½ hours, stirring occasionally. If needed, add a splash of water now and again to prevent the greens from sticking to the bottom of the pan.

Preheat the oven to 200°C/400°F/Gas Mark 6. Grease a baking sheet with oil.

In a large bowl, combine the pumpkin and enough oil to coat. Add the cumin, Aleppo pepper, cinnamon and ½ teaspoon of the salt. Toss to mix, then transfer to the prepared baking sheet. Spread out into a single layer and bake for 30 minutes. Brush with the spicy oil and rose harissa. Roast for another 15 minutes, until caramelised in places. Keep warm.

Meanwhile, remove the pith and flesh from the preserved lime and discard. Finely chop the skin. To the pan of spinach, add the cardamom, beans, preserved lime and 150 ml/5 fl oz (⅔ cup) warm water. Stir for 10 minutes.

Add the lemon zest and juice and the remaining 1 teaspoon of salt. Season to taste with more lemon, salt and pepper if needed.

Spoon into warm bowls, then top with pumpkin wedges. Drizzle with more olive oil. Serve immediately as is or with warm flatbreads or rice, if desired.

TOFU GONDI DUMPLINGS AND BLACK LIME IN TOMATO SAUCE

Serves 4

For the tofu gondi dumplings

30 g/1 oz dried porcini mushrooms, soaked in boiling water

1 x (400-g/14-oz) can red kidney beans, drained and well rinsed

6 Medjool dates, pitted and chopped

4 garlic cloves, finely chopped

4 black limes, finely ground

1 red onion, finely chopped

225 g/8 oz smoked tofu, patted dry with paper towels and coarsely grated

200 g/7 oz (1 cup) cooked basmati rice

30 g/1 oz (½ cup) breadcrumbs

1 tablespoon ground cumin

1 teaspoon ground cardamom

¼ teaspoon ground cinnamon

Salt and black pepper

2 tablespoons extra-virgin olive oil

1 tablespoon dry sherry

Small sprig of dill, leaves only, roughly chopped, to garnish

Seeds from ½ pomegranate, to garnish

For the tomato sauce

1 tablespoon extra-virgin olive oil

2 red onions, thinly sliced

½ teaspoon salt, plus extra

2 garlic cloves, thinly sliced

3 tablespoons tomato purée (paste)

1 x (400-g/14-oz) can chopped tomatoes

1 teaspoon dried mint

1 teaspoon Aleppo pepper

***Gondi* dumplings are a proud culinary tradition of Persian Jews, with every city from Tehran to Shiraz in the southwest claiming that they created the original version. Traditionally made with ground meat and chickpea flour, they're designed for times of gathering and celebration. My *gondi* aren't strictly traditional, but I encourage you to try them.**

Make the tofu gondi dumplings. In a bowl, combine the mushrooms and 475 ml/16 fl oz (2 cups) boiling water. Set aside for 30 minutes.

Using a fork, mash the kidney beans in a large mixing bowl. Add the dates, garlic, black limes, red onion, tofu, cooked rice, breadcrumbs and spices and mix well. Season with salt and pepper.

Remove the mushrooms from the soaking liquid, then squeeze them dry. (Don't be tempted to pour them into a sieve as any grit soaked off the mushrooms will wash back over them.) Discard the liquid. Finely chop the mushrooms.

Heat the oil in a frying pan or skillet over medium heat. Add the mushrooms and sauté for 5 minutes. Remove from the heat and deglaze the pan with the sherry. Stir until all the liquid has been absorbed. Add the mushrooms to the bean-tofu mixture and stir to combine.

Line a baking sheet with parchment paper. Scoop up 50 g/1¾ oz of the mixture and roll it into a ball. The mixture will feel crumbly at first, but will firm up as you squeeze it between your hands. Place it on the prepared baking sheet. Repeat with the remaining mixture; you should get about 20 balls. Chill in the fridge for 1 hour to firm up.

Meanwhile, make the tomato sauce. Heat the oil in a large frying pan or skillet over medium heat, until it shimmers. Add the onions and salt and sauté for 8–10 minutes, until completely softened and golden. Add the garlic and sauté for another minute, until fragrant. Stir in the tomato purée (paste). Mix in the remaining chopped tomatoes, mint and Aleppo pepper. Bring to a boil, then reduce the heat to medium-low and simmer for 20–25 minutes, until the sauce is deep red and the flavour is concentrated. Season to taste with salt.

Preheat the oven to 220°C/425°F/Gas Mark 7. Remove the dumplings from the fridge and bake for 20 minutes until golden.

To serve, spoon the tomato sauce into 4 warm bowls. Carefully top with a few tofu dumplings (they are still very delicate) and garnish with dill and pomegranate.

The tofu dumplings can be made up to 2 days in advance. Uncooked dumplings can be frozen for up to 6 months. When ready to serve, bake from frozen for 24 minutes, until piping hot in the centre.

CELEBRATION PIE

Serves 6

- Extra-virgin olive oil, for frying, brushing and greasing
- 4 red onions, thinly sliced
- 1½ teaspoons salt, plus extra
- 4 garlic cloves, thinly sliced
- 2 bay leaves
- 1 teaspoon Aleppo pepper
- 1 teaspoon coriander seeds
- 1 teaspoon ground cumin
- ½ teaspoon ground cardamom
- 1 x (400-g/14-oz) can chopped tomatoes
- ½ teaspoon sugar
- 150 g/5½ oz (scant ¾ cup) ricotta cheese or silken tofu
- 2 courgettes, sliced into 5-mm/¼-inch lengths
- Black pepper
- Pinch of saffron strands
- 1 teaspoon ground coriander
- 500 g/1 lb 2 oz (2½ cups) cooked freekeh, bulgur wheat, rice or a combination of lentils and grains
- 5 sheets filo (phyllo) pastry
- Green salad or Tomato and Pomegranate Salad (page 74), to serve

This festive, layered pie may require a bit more effort, but you'll be rewarded in spades with smiles around the table. It's special enough for any celebration, but I tend to prepare it for close family and friends as it can be a rather sloppy pie, which only adds to its rustic charm.

Heat 4 tablespoons of the oil in a large frying pan or skillet over medium heat. Add the onions and 1 teaspoon of the salt and sauté for 20 minutes, until the onions are caramelised.

Meanwhile, heat a tablespoon of oil in another saucepan over medium heat, until it shimmers. Add the garlic and sauté for 30 seconds, until fragrant. Add the bay leaf and spices and stir for 30 seconds. Pour in the canned tomatoes, sugar and the remaining salt. Simmer for 15 minutes, stirring occasionally, until the mixture has darkened and reduced by half. Remove from the heat, then stir in the ricotta or tofu.

Heat enough oil to coat the bottom of a large frying pan or skillet over medium heat. Working in batches, add the courgettes (zucchini) and pan-fry for 3 minutes on each side, until golden. Season with salt and pepper. Transfer to a plate and set aside.

In a small mixing bowl, combine the saffron, coriander and 1 tablespoon of boiling water.

Heat 3 tablespoons of oil in a small pan over medium-high heat. Add the cooked grains and stir well, until warmed through. Transfer the grains to a mixing bowl, then stir in the saffron mixture.

Grease a 23-cm/9-inch springform pan and lay 3 sheets of filo (phyllo) in the pan, overlapping them at angles and brushing oil between each layer. Add the caramelised red onions and spread out, pressing down with the back of a spoon. Transfer about 80 per cent of the grain mixture into the pan. Again, use the back of the spoon to press down and compact the grains. Lay the courgette slices over the top of the grains to completely cover them and meet the edge of the filo (phyllo) pastry. Pour over the tomato sauce, then add the remaining grains. Top with the remaining filo, pinching and arranging so the pastry is wavy. Brush with olive oil. Chill in the refrigerator.

Preheat the oven to 200°C/400°F/Gas Mark 6.

Bake the pie for 45 minutes, until golden and crisp all over. Set aside for 10 minutes to cool in the pan.

Carefully run a palette knife around the edges to release the pie. Remove the sides, then carefully slide the pie off the base and onto a cooling rack. Cool for 15 minutes. (The cooling time will help the pie to keep its shape when sliced.)

Slice into wedges with a serrated knife. Serve with salad.

BREADS

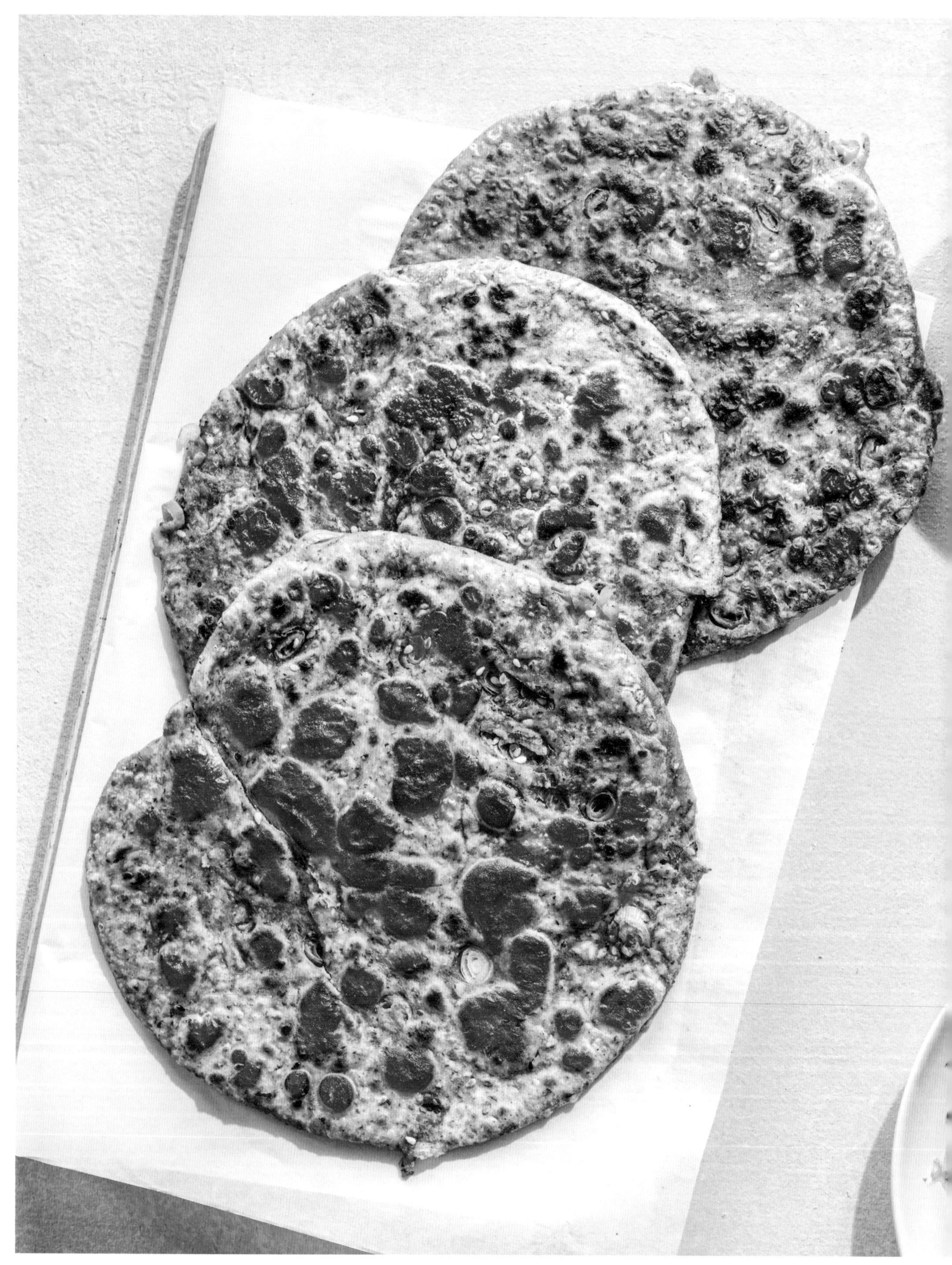

L–R Spinach Kulcha (page 208), Taboon Bread (page 209).

NF

HERB AND FETA FLATBREAD

Makes 6

For the dough

400 g/14 oz (3¼ cups) strong white bread flour, plus extra for dusting

5 tablespoons olive oil, plus extra for greasing

1 teaspoon salt

For the filling

Vegetable oil, for frying

Bunch of spring onions (scallions), roughly chopped

3 garlic cloves, finely chopped

150 g/5½ oz parsley, finely chopped

100 g/3½ oz dill, finely chopped

50 g/1¾ oz coriander (cilantro), finely chopped

100 g/3½ oz crumbled feta

150 g/5½ oz (1½ cups) grated mozzarella

1 teaspoon ground coriander

¼ teaspoon nutmeg

½ teaspoon salt

Black pepper

1 egg, beaten

In Turkey, *gözleme* are paper-thin flatbreads stuffed with everything from lamb to spinach. Here, I use the herbs like a vegetable (which is common across the Middle East), cooking big bunches of chopped leaves and stems until just wilted. Then, I combine it with two cheeses for contrast.

It's a fairly versatile recipe, so use whatever you have in the refrigerator and stick to the quantity guidelines below.

Make the dough. In a large mixing bowl, combine all the ingredients. Pour in 210 ml/7¼ fl oz (¾ cup plus 2 tablespoons) lepid water. With clean hands, mix for 3 minutes, until the mixture comes together in a ball. Pull the dough to one side of the bowl, and pour a little olive oil into the bottom of the bowl to grease. Cover and set aside to rest for 30 minutes.

Meanwhile, make the filling. Heat a tablespoon of oil in a large frying pan or skillet over medium heat. Add the spring onions (scallions) and gently sauté for 3 minutes, until translucent. Add the garlic and sauté for another minute, until fragrant. Stir in the herbs. Stir in the feta, mozzarella and spices. Season to taste with the salt and pepper. Stir in the egg, then set aside.

Preheat the oven to 200°C/400°F/Gas Mark 6. Line 2 baking sheets with parchment paper.

Cut the dough into 6 equal-sized pieces. Roll out each piece on a lightly floured surface until roughly 25 cm/10 inches in diameter. Place a sixth of the filling in the centre of each piece of dough. Fold the outside into the centre in 6 stages, so there is a fanned overlap of the dough to seal in the filling. Gently roll out until each stuffed dough is a rough 20-cm/8-inch circle.

Heat 2 tablespoons of oil in a large frying pan or skillet over medium heat. Working in batches to avoid overcrowding, pan-fry the stuffed doughs for 3 minutes on each side. Transfer to the prepared baking sheets. Bake for 10–12 minutes, until piping hot.

Serve warm with a cold drink.

TURKISH SESAME BREAD

Makes 4

300 g/10½ oz (2⅓ cups) strong white bread flour, plus extra for dusting
2 teaspoons fast-action (active dry) yeast
1 teaspoon sugar
1 teaspoon salt
3 tablespoons date syrup
Olive oil, for greasing
100 g/3½ oz (scant ½ cup) sesame seeds

I'll be the first to readily admit that I have a sweet tooth, and this bread checks all the boxes. The date syrup lends a subtle sweetness, making this bread perfect alongside pickles, jams or a quality extra-virgin olive oil.

Known as *simit*, these decorative breads are best for tearing when they're still warm from the oven – the irregular edges create the ideal vessel for your favourite toppings.

In a large bowl, combine the flour, yeast, sugar, salt and 2 tablespoons of the date syrup. Make a well in the centre, then pour in 175 ml/6 fl oz (¾ cup) of tepid water. With clean hands, bring the mixture together into a ball in the bowl. This should take 2–3 minutes.

Lightly dust a clean work surface, then turn the dough out onto it. Knead for 10 minutes, until the dough is smooth and bounces back when poked with your index finger. Place in a lightly oiled mixing bowl, cover with a dish towel and set aside in a warm place for 1½–2 hours until the dough has doubled in size.

Line a baking sheet with parchment paper.

Lay the sesame seeds on a plate. In a wide, shallow bowl, mix the remaining 1 tablespoon of date syrup and 3 tablespoons hot water.

Remove the dough from the bowl, cut into 4 equal pieces and roll a piece with your hands into a long sausage shape, about 2.5 cm/1 inch wide. Pull the dough into a V with the centre point closest to you and the 2 ends furthest away from you. Twist the 2 sides of rope over and under each other to plait (braid) it, then lightly dampen the 2 ends with the date syrup and water mixture and pinch together to join, leaving a palm-sized cavity in the centre. Dip the plaited (braided) dough in the date mixture, then coat both sides in the sesame seeds. Transfer to the prepared baking sheet. Repeat with the remaining dough. Cover with a clean dish towel to prove (proof) for 45 minutes.

Preheat the oven to 200°C/400°F/Gas Mark 6.

Bake for 20 minutes, until golden. Serve immediately.

Leftover bread can be stored in an airtight container for 2 days. Gently reheat before serving.

LEBANESE FLATBREAD

Makes 8

- 7g/ ¼ oz fast-action (active dry) yeast
- 1 teaspoon sugar
- 375 g/13 oz (3 cups plus 1 tablespoon) strong white bread flour, plus extra for dusting
- 2 teaspoons salt
- 1 tablespoon extra virgin olive oil, plus extra for greasing
- Roasted Carrot Mezze (page 180) or Tomato and Mint Mezze (page 173), to serve

No true Lebanese meal is complete without a pillowy flatbread for scooping sauces and mopping up juices.

I prepare this trusted recipe all the time, serving it multiple times a week with pickles and hummus or curries and lentil dishes. Be sure to serve these fresh and warm or refresh in a low oven up to 3 days after making them.

In a small bowl, combine the yeast, sugar and 160 ml/5½ fl oz (⅔ cup) tepid water and stir until the yeast and sugar have dissolved. Set aside for 10 minutes, until frothy.

In a large bowl, combine the flour and salt. Make a well in the centre, then pour in the foamy yeast mixture and olive oil. With clean hands, knead the dough in the bowl for 5 minutes, or until it comes together in a shaggy ball. Lightly grease the bottom of the bowl, then nestle the dough in the centre. Cover with a clean dish towel and set aside for 1 hour in a warm place, until doubled in size.

Preheat a griddle pan over medium heat for 10 minutes.

Place the dough on a lightly floured surface. Knead for 5 minutes, until the dough is smooth. Divide into 8 equal pieces, then roll out to 3-mm/⅛-inch thick discs. One by one, pan-fry the flatbread for 4 minutes on each side, only moving them to flip, until the dough is no longer grey and they are marked with black stripes on each side.

Serve the flatbreads with either mezze.

LAYERED GARLIC AND SESAME FLATBREAD

Makes 8

2 teaspoons fast-action (active dry) yeast

1 tablespoon sugar

450 g/1 lb (3½ cups) strong white bread flour, plus extra for dusting

2 teaspoons salt

4 tablespoons extra-virgin olive oil, plus extra for greasing

6 garlic cloves, crushed to a paste

3 tablespoons tahini

Sesame seeds, for sprinkling

These breads are full of flavour from the tahini and garlic, which are folded between layers of the dough in a process similar to making rough puff pastry. This folding of fat (tahini and oil) between dough creates the visible layers in the bread when it's broken into.

In a jug (pitcher), combine the yeast, sugar and 200 ml/7 fl oz (¾ cup plus 1 tablespoon) tepid water. Stir until the yeast has dissolved, then set aside for 8–10 minutes, until foamy.

Combine the flour and salt in a large bowl and mix. Add 2 tablespoons of the oil and mix until combined. (The flour will look lumpy.) Make a well in the centre, then slowly pour in the yeast mixture. With clean hands, knead the dough in the bowl until the mixture forms a shaggy ball. Transfer the dough to a lightly floured surface and knead for 10 minutes, until the dough bounces back when poked. Transfer the dough back to the mixing bowl, lightly oiled this time, and cover with a clean dish towel. Set aside in a warm place for 1 hour, or until doubled in size.

Meanwhile, in a small bowl, combine the garlic, tahini and the remaining 2 tablespoons of oil.

Lightly dust the work surface again. Using a rolling pin, roll out the dough to a thin and translucent 80 × 50-cm/30 × 20-inch rectangle. Add more flour as needed to prevent it from sticking – it sounds a bit messy, but it prevents the dough from tearing. With clean fingers, spread the tahini and garlic mixture, leaving a 1-cm/½-inch border. Carefully roll the dough into a tight roulade, along the longer end. Using a dough scraper, cut into 8 × 10-cm/4-inch-wide pieces.

Grease a baking sheet. Take one piece of dough. Tuck both cut sides underneath and pinch to seal, so none of the tahini filling is visible. Using the rolling pin, roll the dough out on a lightly floured surface to a 20-cm/8-inch square. Fold the top half down and the bottom half up to meet in the middle with plenty of overlap, then fold in the sides in the same way. Flip the dough over so the seam is on the bottom. Roll out the dough to 10 × 7.5 cm/4 × 3 inches. Brush with water and sprinkle with the sesame seeds. Place on the prepared baking sheet. Repeat with the remaining dough, evenly spacing the dough on the baking sheet 2 cm/¾ inch apart. Cover with a clean dish towel, then set aside to prove (proof) for 30 minutes in a warm place.

Preheat the oven to 200°C/400°F/Gas Mark 6. Bake the flatbreads for 15–17 minutes, until puffed up and deep golden. Transfer to a cooling rack for 15 minutes. Serve warm.

Leftover flatbreads can be heated through in a warm oven up to 3 days after baking.

ZA'ATAR PARATHAS

Makes 8

For the parathas

400 g/14 oz (3⅓ cups) strong white bread flour, plus extra for dusting

1 tablespoon salt

2 tablespoons vegetable oil , plus extra for greasing

Semolina (farina), for dusting

4 tablespoons ghee, softened, plus extra for brushing

4 tablespoons Za'atar (page 254)

For the date and tamarind chutney

4 Medjool dates, pitted and soaked in boiling water

80 g/2¾ oz tamarind pulp, soaked in 100 ml/3½ fl oz (scant ½ cup) boiling water

Small thumb-sized piece of fresh ginger, grated

3 mastic grains, crushed in a pestle and mortar

Pinch of salt, plus extra

Lemon juice (optional)

This is an impressive dish which truly bridges the Middle East and the Indian subcontinent. The spirals flake apart to reveal a delicious za'atar filling. The date chutney is a perfect accompaniment and comes together in 5 minutes.

Make the parathas. In a large bowl, combine the flour and salt and mix well. Make a well in the centre, then pour in the vegetable oil. Rub the oil and flour between your fingers until the mixture resembles breadcrumbs. Make a well in the centre and slowly pour in 225 ml/7½ fl oz (scant 1 cup) warm water.

With your hands, bring the dough together in the bowl, until it forms a ball. Transfer to a clean work surface dusted with semolina (farina) and knead for 5 minutes, until the dough is smooth and not sticky. Grease a bowl, add the dough and cover with a damp dish towel. Set aside for 2 hours to rest.

Place 85 g/3 oz of the dough on a floured surface. Using a rolling pin, roll out to a thin circle, about 25 cm/10 inches in diameter.

Using a rubber spatula or dough scraper, spread ½ tablespoon of the softened ghee over the thin disc. Sprinkle over ½ tablespoon of the za'atar. Sprinkle over a pinch of flour, then carefully roll the disc from the side furthest away from you towards you to create a log shape. Coil the dough and place on a baking sheet lined with parchment paper. Repeat with the remaining dough, ghee and za'atar. Set aside to rest for 30 minutes.

Meanwhile, make the chutney. Drain the dates, then add to a food processor. Press down on the tamarind in the water to dissolve as much of the pulp into the water as possible. The liquid should be the thickness of double (heavy) cream. Drain the tamarind through a fine-mesh sieve into the food processor and discard the seeds. Add the ginger, mastic and salt. Blitz until smooth, then season to taste with lemon juice or more salt. Transfer to a bowl.

Lightly dust a clean work surface with flour. Roll out a paratha to a 20-cm/8-inch disc, dusting the rolling pin and surface with flour as you go. Repeat with the remaining parathas, stacking them between parchment paper.

Heat a frying pan or skillet over medium heat. Pan-fry the parathas, one at a time, for 3–4 minutes on each side until golden spots form all over. Transfer to a plate and stack the parathas between the same parchment again.

Brush each cooked paratha with ghee, then pan-fry again, one by one, for 2 minutes each side until crisp. Wrap in a clean dish towel and keep warm in a low oven until the rest are cooked. Serve immediately with the chutney.

LEBANESE RING BREAD

Makes 4

300 g/10½ oz (2½ cups) strong white bread flour
1 teaspoon sugar
1 teaspoon salt
2 teaspoons fast-action (active dry) yeast
2 tablespoons extra-virgin olive oil, plus extra for greasing
3 tablespoons milk
100 g/3½ oz (scant ½ cup) sesame seeds

The shape of this bread, known as *ka'ek*, will vary, depending on where you are in the region. Whether it's a thick-bottom bread shaped like a handbag or an elongated oval, one thing remains the same: a hole in the centre.

Typically, vendors loop fresh *ka'eks* on a stick and walk the busy streets in the morning to sell the bread to commuters and families. It's best served warm with grassy olive oil for dipping, creamy sharp labneh for spreading and za'atar for sprinkling.

In a large mixing bowl, combine the flour, sugar, salt, yeast and olive oil. Make a well in the centre and pour in 175 ml/6 fl oz (¾ cup) tepid water. Mix with a wooden spoon, until it forms a dough. Transfer to a clean work surface and knead for 10 minutes, until the dough is smooth and elastic.

Lightly oil the same mixing bowl (there's no need to wash it out) and add the dough. Cover with a clean dish towel and leave for 1 hour in a warm place until doubled in size.

Line a baking sheet with parchment paper. Divide the dough into 4 balls. Roll each ball out into a log, about 15 cm/6 inches long. Moisten the ends of the dough with water and bring together into a ring with a hole in the middle.

Transfer the dough to the prepared baking sheet. Brush the dough with milk, then sprinkle over the sesame seeds. Cover with a dish towel and prove for another 30 minutes.

Preheat the oven to 200°C/400°F/Gas Mark 6. Bake for 22–25 minutes, until puffed and golden.

Serve warm. Leftover bread can be stored in an airtight container for up to 3 days. Warm in a low oven before serving.

MANAKISH

Dimpled *manakish* are famed for their wobbly surface (the root of the word means to 'engrave' or 'carve out'). Like pizza, *manakish* offer seemingly endless topping possibilities, but the most common are za'atar and oil and melted cheese.

I like to prepare a few topping options and allow guests to choose their own.

Makes 6

7g/ ¼ oz fast-action (active dry) yeast

1 teaspoon sugar

325 g/11½ oz (2¾ cups) strong white bread flour, plus extra for dusting

1 teaspoon salt

3 tablespoons extra-virgin olive oil

For the toppings

Za'atar (page 254) and olive oil

Sliced tomatoes and olives

Grated halloumi cheese and wilted spinach or dried mint

In a bowl, combine the yeast, sugar and 190 ml/7 fl oz (scant 1 cup) tepid water. Stir to combine, then set aside until the yeast has started to foam (about 10 minutes).

Mix the flour and salt together in a large mixing bowl, make a well in the centre and pour in the oil and water mixture. Bring together with your hands in the bowl before turning out onto a surface dusted with flour to knead for 10 minutes until smooth and bouncy.

Cover and set aside in a warm place to rise for an hour.

Preheat the oven to 200°C/400°F/Gas Mark 6. Divide the dough into 6 and roll into balls. Use a rolling pin to roll out to 1 cm/½ inch thickness, about 15 cm/6 inches diameter. Top with your chosen topping, or a mixture of all 3 and bake, in batches if needed on a parchment paper-lined baking sheet for 12 minutes until golden. Drizzle with olive oil before serving.

SPINACH KULCHA

Makes 8

100 g/3½ oz (3⅓ cups) spinach
1 tablespoon Za'atar (page 254)
1 teaspoon ground cumin
1 teaspoon salt
350 g/12 oz (1½ cups) Greek yogurt
450 g/1 lb (3⅔ cups) self-raising flour, sifted, plus extra for dusting
2 tablespoons sesame seeds
Small bunch of spring onions (scallions), thinly sliced
Small bunch of coriander (cilantro), leaves only
Ghee, for frying

These stuffed yogurt flatbreads, known as *kulcha*, originated in northern India, and their popularity spread across the Levant. Typically stuffed with mashed potato, I've opted to omit the potatoes and create a version with spinach and za'atar mixed into the dough. It's much easier and makes for a striking dough.

Any leftover flatbreads can be frozen in sealed bags after cooking and gently reheated in a low oven until warmed through. Serve it with soups, chickpea dishes or stews.

In a food processor, combine the spinach, za'atar, cumin, salt and yogurt and blend until smooth.

Place the flour in a large mixing bowl and make a well in the centre. Using a rubber spatula, scrape out the spinach-yogurt mixture into the bowl and mix to combine. Cover and set aside to rest for 1 hour.

Divide the dough into 8. On a lightly floured work surface, roll out a piece of dough using a floured rolling pin, until it measures about 20 cm/8 inches in diameter. Dust both sides of the dough with flour as you go. Sprinkle over about ¾ teaspoon of sesame seeds, spring onions (scallions) and coriander (cilantro). From one end to the opposite, roll the dough up into a tight Swiss roll shape. Roll it up again, starting at one long end, into a tight ball. Lightly dust the dough and rolling pin, then roll out to about 18 cm/7 inches in diameter. Repeat with the remaining dough, sesame seeds, spring onions and coriander.

Heat a teaspoon of ghee in a large frying pan or skillet over medium heat. Working with one at a time, add a flatbread to the pan. Pan-fry for 5–7 minutes on each side, until golden all over. Transfer to a plate and keep warm. Repeat with the remaining *kulchas*, adding more ghee after each one.

Serve immediately.

Photo on page 194.

TABOON BREAD

Makes 8

2½ teaspoons fast-action (active dry) yeast

Pinch of sugar

540 g/1 lb 3½ oz (4½ cups) strong white bread flour, plus extra for dusting

1 tablespoon salt

3 tablespoons olive oil, plus extra for greasing

This pillowy bread gets its name from the oven it's cooked in, like an Indian *tandoor* oven. As they're not commonplace in domestic kitchens, I suggest you cook these on a pizza stone or cast-iron pan that has been preheated in the oven. If you don't own either of those, use the bottom of a baking sheet. It won't have the exact same effect, but it will help the dough to rise as it cooks.

I use this bread instead of a wrap or as a base to the saucy Musakhan on page 166.

Preheat a pizza stone, large cast-iron frying pan or baking sheet in a 220°C/425°F/Gas Mark 7 oven.

In a jug (pitcher), combine the yeast, sugar and 325 ml/11 fl oz (1¼ cups plus 2 tablespoons) tepid water. Stir until the yeast has dissolved. Set aside for 10 minutes, until foamy.

Meanwhile, in a large mixing bowl, combine the flour and salt. Pour in the olive oil and rub it between your fingers until the mixture resembles breadcrumbs. Make a well in the centre of the flour. Pour in the yeast mixture. With clean hands, bring the mixture together, until a ball forms.

Lightly dust a clean work surface with flour. Knead with your hands for 10 minutes, stretching, folding and bringing the dough together, until it becomes smooth and elastic. Lightly grease the bowl, then add the dough. Cover with a clean dish towel and set aside for 1–1½ hours, until it has doubled in size.

Cut into 8 even pieces, then roll out to a 15-cm/6-inch diameter. Bake the dough in batches of 2 or 3 (so there is no overlap) for 7–8 minutes, until puffed up and golden.

Serve warm. Leftover taboon bread can be stored in an airtight container for up to 3 days. Warm before serving.

Photo on page 195.

SPRING ONION AND HERB ROTI

Makes 6

250 g/9 oz (scant 1⅔ cups) plain (all-purpose) flour, plus extra for dusting
1 teaspoon fine salt
½ teaspoon baking powder
1 tablespoon ghee or vegetable oil, melted, plus extra for frying
1 heaped teaspoon Za'atar (page 254)
4 spring onions (scallions), finely chopped
½ small bunch parsley, leaves only, roughly chopped
Pickles, Aubergine and Yogurt Mezze (page 18) or Spinach Borani with Walnuts (page 172), to serve

Roti breads are unleavened breads, originally from India. With more and more people moving across borders, they are now sold on street corners and stalls around the Levant and adapted for local tastes, such as this za'atar-laced version.

Fried in ghee, they're flakier than baked breads and quicker to make as they require no rising time. The rolled doughs can be frozen between layers of parchment paper in a sealable plastic bag, then cooked from frozen for 5–6 minutes.

In a large bowl, combine the flour, salt and baking powder. Add a tablespoon of ghee or oil and rub the mixture together between your fingers. Make a well in the centre and slowly pour in 150 ml/ 5 fl oz (⅔ cup) tepid water. Scatter over the za'atar, spring onions (scallions) and parsley. With clean hands, mix to form a dough. Cover, then set aside for 30 minutes to rest.

Lightly dust a clean work surface with flour. Divide the dough into 6 balls. Dust a rolling pin with flour, then roll out each ball into an 18-cm/7-inch disc.

Heat a tablespoon of ghee in a heavy frying pan or skillet over medium heat for 2 minutes. Add a roti to the pan and pan-fry for 3–4 minutes each side, until crisp, deep golden and charred in places. Repeat with the remaining roti, adding more ghee each time.

Serve immediately alongside pickles, aubergine and yogurt mezze or spinach borani.

ZA'ATAR GARLIC BREAD

Serves 4

1 par-baked baguette, sliced in half lengthwise
75 g/2¾ oz butter, softened
4 garlic cloves, crushed
¼ bunch of parsley, leaves only, finely chopped
2 teaspoons Za'atar (page 254), plus extra for sprinkling
Salt and black pepper
75 g/2¾ oz (¾ cup) grated mozzarella (optional)

Thanks to its woody, savoury and sharp flavour, za'atar is as essential a seasoning as salt and pepper. We Lebanese sprinkle it on so many savoury dishes.

I urge you to try this twist on traditional Italian garlic bread. It's perfect as a snack before dinner, or alongside savoury, saucy dishes.

Preheat the oven to 200°C/400°F/Gas Mark 6.

Using a serrated knife, cut 10 incisions into the cut side of the baguette, stopping halfway down. This should give you 10 little cavities in the baguette.

In a bowl, combine the butter, garlic, parsley and za'atar. Mix well with a fork. Season with salt and pepper.

Using a teaspoon, place the za'atar butter into the incisions. Add the mozzarella, if using. Wrap the baguette tightly in aluminium foil, cut side up.

Bake for 15 minutes. Open up the foil to expose the top of the baguette and bake for another 15 minutes, until crisp and golden. Sprinkle with more za'atar.

Serve warm.

The baguette can be sliced, filled and chilled up to 2 days before baking. Alternatively, slice, fill and wrap it in clingfilm (plastic wrap) and freeze for up to 3 months. Defrost completely before baking.

DESSERTS

L–R Persian Toffee Brittle (page 230), Coconut Cookies (page 231).

FAVOURITE BAKLAVA

Makes about 3 dozen

For the baklava

200 g/7 oz (1¾ cups) blanched almonds
160 g/5½ oz (1 cup) pistachios, plus 3 tablespoons to decorate
175 g/6 oz (scant 1 cup) sugar
½ teaspoon ground cardamom
¼ teaspoon ground cinnamon
⅛ teaspoon allspice
Small pinch of salt
150 g/5½ oz butter, melted
12 sheets filo (phyllo) pastry
150 g/5½ oz (⅔ cup) runny honey
1 teaspoon rosewater
Grated zest and juice of 1 lemon
Grated zest of 1 orange

Is there any Middle Eastern sweet more iconic than baklava? I struggle these days to find a corner shop that doesn't sell a pack of these sticky sweet pastries by the till.

Although there are numerous variations, this is my favourite flavour combination: buttery nuts, gentle spicing and sweet citrus syrup.

Make the baklava. Preheat the oven to 160°C/325°F/Gas Mark 3.

In a food processor, combine the nuts, 2 tablespoons of the sugar, the spices and salt and process until a rough crumb forms.

Brush the inside edges of a large baking pan with melted butter. Lay a sheet of filo (phyllo) across the base. Fold in any overhanging edges of filo to form a neat rectangle within the pan's edges. Brush the top of the filo with butter. Repeat with 3 more sheets of filo, brushing with melted butter as you go.

Add half of the nut mixture on top and spread out evenly. Lay 4 more sheets of pastry over the nuts, brushing each one with melted butter. Spread out the remaining nuts. Finish the baklava with a final 4 layers of filo, brushing each with more melted butter. Cut the pastry into diamonds or squares (slicing right through to the bottom of the pan), about 4 cm/1½ inches wide. Bake for 50 minutes, until puffed and golden.

Meanwhile, make the syrup. In a small saucepan, combine the remaining sugar, honey, rosewater, lemon juice and citrus zests. Pour in 100 ml/3½ fl oz (scant ½ cup) water and cook over medium heat, until it turns to a deep caramel-coloured syrup.

Remove the baklava from the oven and immediately pour over the syrup. (If the syrup has cooled down and hardened, warm it through to make it runny.)

Chop the remaining pistachios into slivers and place in the centre of each square or diamond. Set the baklava aside for 15 minutes.

Transfer to a plate and serve.

Baklava can be stored in an airtight container for up to a week.

GRILLED PEACHES AND TOASTED SESAME SHORTBREAD

Serves 10–12

200 g/7 oz butter, softened, plus extra for greasing

100 g/3½ oz (½ cup) golden sugar

2 teaspoons rosewater

200 g/7 oz (1¼ cups) plain (all-purpose) flour

100 g/3½ oz (scant 1 cup) cornflour (cornstarch)

1 teaspoon salt

2 tablespoons rose sugar or golden sugar, plus extra for the peaches

3 tablespoons sesame seeds, toasted

5–6 peaches, cut in half and stoned

Edible rose petals, to decorate (optional)

1 tablespoon ground pistachios (optional)

Depending on the season, you can make this with different fruits – try roasted strawberries in the early summer, pan-caramelised blood orange segments in the winter and plums in autumn.

Rose sugar can be purchased in Middle Eastern shops or online. Fresh rose petals make for a pretty decoration, too.

Preheat the oven to 150°C/300°F/Gas Mark 2. Generously grease a 20 × 30-cm/8 × 12 inch baking pan or 22 cm/8½-inch round cake pan.

In a large bowl, beat the butter and golden sugar together with an electric whisk until light and fluffy. Stir in the rosewater, then fold in the plain (all-purpose) flour, cornflour (cornstarch) and salt. Whisk on a slow speed, until the mixture resembles coarse crumbs and comes together when you pinch it between your fingers.

Press the shortbread mixture into the prepared pan, pressing it down with the back of a wooden spoon so that it's compacted and level. Pierce all over with a fork. Bake for 55 minutes, until lightly golden and firm to the touch.

Using a sharp knife, immediately slice the shortbread into fingers, squares or wedges. Scatter with the rose or golden sugar and sesame seeds. Set aside to cool completely.

Preheat the grill (broiler) to its highest setting. Place the peaches, cut side up, on a roasting pan and sprinkle the sugar on top. Grill for 4–5 minutes, until golden, bubbling and soft.

Plate the shortbread biscuits with the peaches. Sprinkle with rose petals and ground pistachio, if using, and serve.

KNAFEH

Serves 4

230 g/8 oz kataifi pastry, thawed if frozen
115 g/4 oz butter, melted
250 g/9 oz (2½ cups) grated mozzarella
75 g/2¾ oz (⅓ cup) ricotta
225 g/8 oz (1 cup plus 2 tablespoons) sugar
Grated zest and juice of 1 lemon
1 tablespoon rosewater
50 g/1¾ oz (⅓ cup) pistachios, chopped
1 tablespoon edible dried rose petals

This popular Middle Eastern dessert is easy to make, once you get your head around the fact that the pastry looks like a thin noodle. It is traditionally made with akawi (a salty Middle Eastern cheese), which requires 48 hours of soaking time to draw out the salt. Instead, I have suggested a more readily available mozzarella for a similar result.

If you like, feel free to use akawi cheese, which can be purchased at Middle Eastern shops. Just be sure to soak it for 48 hours, changing the water every 12 hours.

Preheat the oven to 200°C/400°F/Gas Mark 6.

In a bowl, combine the pastry and melted butter. With clean hands, separate the strands and distribute the butter evenly among the pastry.

Pack half of the buttery pastry into the bottom of a 23-cm/9-inch tart pan, making sure some of the pastry covers the side. Using the bottom of a glass, gently press the pastry to pack it down tightly.

In a separate mixing bowl, combine the mozzarella and ricotta. Add the cheese mixture to the pan and spread out over the pastry. Cover with 2 tablespoons of the sugar and the remaining pastry. Pack down again with the glass. Bake for 25 minutes, until crisp and golden.

Meanwhile, make the syrup. In a saucepan, combine the remaining sugar, lemon zest and juice, rosewater and 200 ml/7 fl oz (¾ cup plus 1 tablespoon) water. Bring to a boil, then reduce the heat to medium-low and simmer for 8–10 minutes, until syrupy.

When the pastry is cooked, pour over the syrup. Set aside to rest for 5 minutes, then invert onto a plate.

Top with the chopped pistachios and rose petals. Slice and serve.

FOUR SEASONS FROZEN LABNEH YOGURT

Serves 6

900 g/2 lb (4 cups) Greek yogurt
300 g/10½ oz Seasonal Fruits (see below)
3–5 tablespoons sugar
2 fresh bay leaves
100 g/3½ oz (⅔ cup) honey
Fresh fruit or Persian Toffee Brittle (page 230), to serve

Seasonal fruits

Spring	Rhubarb, trimmed into 1-cm/½-inch pieces
Summer	Strawberries, halved
Autumn	Plums, cored and roughly chopped
Winter	Persimmons, roughly chopped, or frozen mixed berries

No part of the world has embraced the versatility of yogurt more than the Middle East. Here, I ripple seasonal fruits through thick labneh and freeze it for my own take on frozen yogurt, which is lighter than dairy ice cream.

The drained yogurt whey can be used instead of water in bread doughs – it introduces a lovely tang to sourdoughs and flatbreads.

Line a colander with a piece of muslin (cheesecloth) and suspend the colander over a bowl. Add the yogurt to the colander, gather up the muslin sides to seal and drain the yogurt at room temperature for 4 hours. (The watery whey in the bowl can be used to make bread or replace filtered water when preserving vegetables.) Transfer the labneh to a mixing bowl.

An hour before the yogurt straining time is up, arrange the seasonal fruit in a saucepan in an even layer. Sprinkle over 3 tablespoons of the sugar for the summer or autumn fruit, or 5 tablespoons for winter or spring fruit. Add the bay leaves and 3 tablespoons of water. Poach gently over medium heat until tender. Soft fruits will cook quickly, whereas the rhubarb may require up to 15 minutes. Set aside to cool completely.

Line a 900-g/2-lb loaf pan with clingfilm (plastic wrap) on all sides.

Pour the labneh into a large mixing bowl and stir in the honey. Using a rubber spatula, mix in the fruit and its juices in no more than 4 turns. The fruit and juices should be rippled through the labneh.

Pour the flavoured labneh into the prepared loaf pan, levelling out the top with a rubber spatula. Cover with clingfilm and chill in the freezer for 4–5 hours. Using the clingfilm, lift out the frozen yogurt from the pan and invert onto a serving plate.

Slice, then serve with fresh fruit or brittle.

NF

LITTLE DONUT BALLS

Serves 8

For the donut balls

600 g/1 lb 5 oz (3¾ cups) plain (all-purpose) flour

10 g/¼ oz fast-action (active dry) instant yeast

Pinch of salt

70 g/2½ oz butter

70 g/2½ oz (⅓ cup) sugar

450 ml/15 fl oz (1⅔ cups plus 2 tablespoons) milk

3 whole eggs

1 egg yolk

Sunflower oil, for frying

For the sugar syrup

200 g/7 oz (1 cup) sugar

1 bay leaf

Grated zest and juice of 1 lemon

1 tablespoon rosewater

These little donuts are based on *awamat,* Lebanese donuts drizzled in simple syrup. They make a great dessert centrepiece with ice cream or fresh fruit – just be sure to eat them on the day they're made as they are best served fresh and warm.

I drizzle these in sugar syrup, but you could toss them in sugar (like traditional American donuts without the hole).

Make the donut balls. In a mixing bowl, combine the flour, yeast and salt.

Put the butter in a separate bowl.

Combine the sugar and milk in a saucepan and heat gently, until the sugar has dissolved. Do not boil. Pour the hot milk over the butter. Set aside until lukewarm. Whisk in the eggs and yolk.

Pour the wet mixture into the dry. Stir, using a wooden spoon until the batter is smooth. Cover the bowl with a clean dish towel and set aside in a warm place for 1 hour, or until doubled in size.

Meanwhile, make the syrup. Combine the sugar and bay leaf in a saucepan. Pour in 200 ml/7 fl oz (¾ cup plus 1 tablespoon) of water. Bring to a boil, then reduce the heat to medium-low and gently simmer for 8–10 minutes, until the syrup has slightly thickened and the bubbles are large and glossy. Set aside to cool for 3 minutes. Stir in the lemon zest and juice and rosewater.

Heat the oil in a large saucepan, to a depth of 10 cm/4 inches, over medium heat. The oil is ready when a cube of bread dropped in sizzles on contact and turns golden in 35 seconds. (Alternatively, use a thermometer and heat to 160°C/325°F.)

Using 2 spoons, shape the dough into balls, about 4 cm/1½ inches in diameter. Working in small batches to avoid overcrowding, gently lower the dough balls into the hot oil. Deep-fry for 30 seconds, then turn over and deep-fry for another 30 seconds, until golden brown. Using a slotted spoon, transfer to a paper towel–lined plate. Repeat with the remaining donuts.

Drizzle over the warm syrup, then set aside for 3 minutes so that the donuts can absorb the syrup. Serve immediately.

NO-CHURN TAHINI-ESPRESSO ICE CREAM

Makes 750 ml/25 fl oz (3 cups)

425 ml/15 fl oz (1¾ cups) double (heavy) cream
½ teaspoon vanilla bean paste or extract
¼ teaspoon flaky sea salt
1 x (397-g/14-oz) can condensed milk
125 ml/4 fl oz (½ cup) very strong coffee or espresso
3 tablespoons tahini

Pictured opposite.

Once you've discovered how easy it is to make no-churn ice cream, you'll wonder why you ever made it any other way. Condensed milk seems to have fallen out of favour as an ingredient in recent years, but it's the key to the richness and sweetness of this ice cream.

In a large bowl, combine the cream, vanilla and salt. Using an electric whisk, whisk until the mixture resembles Greek yogurt. Add the condensed milk, coffee and tahini. Mix again until it has the consistency of Greek yogurt.

Transfer the mixture to a freezer-safe container and cover with clingfilm (plastic wrap) or beeswax wrap. Place in the freezer for at least 8 hours, or overnight.

Defrost the ice cream for 5 minutes, then serve.

The ice cream can be stored in the freezer for 3 months.

MULBERRY, ORANGE AND SESAME SEED BRITTLE

Serves 8

2 tablespoons dried mulberries
1½ tablespoons sultanas or golden raisins
Juice of 2 oranges
100 g/3½ oz (scant ½ cup) sesame seeds
125 g/4¼ oz (⅔ cup) sugar
Pinch of flaky sea salt
Grated zest of 1 orange

Mulberries are symbolically significant in Persian culture, representing joy and prosperity. Fresh mulberries are prized and have a short season, so dried mulberries are more common. Find them in wholefood shops or online.

Serve this brittle on top of yogurt or ice cream.

In a bowl, combine the mulberries, sultanas and orange juice. Set aside to soak for 1 hour, until plump.

Drain the fruit, reserving the soaking liquid. Transfer the fruit to a food processor and blitz until smooth. Set aside.

Lay parchment paper over a work surface, ready for the brittle.

Toast the sesame seeds in a frying pan or skillet over medium heat for 3 minutes, until some turn golden. Add the reserved soaking liquid, sugar and salt. Stir for 5 minutes, until the sugar has caramelised. Remove from the heat, then stir in the zest and blitzed fruit. Return the pan to the heat and clip a sugar thermometer to the side. Cook until the mixture reaches 140°C/284°F.

Carefully scrape the mixture onto the parchment paper. Using a rubber spatula, even it out to a 2-mm/¹⁄₁₆-inch thickness. Set aside for 1 hour, until hardened. Break into shards.

PERSIAN TOFFEE BRITTLE

Serves 8

225 g/8 oz (1 cup plus 2 tablespoons) sugar
1 tablespoon plain (all-purpose) flour
50 g/1¾ oz butter
3 tablespoons golden syrup or corn syrup
3 strands saffron, ground with a pinch of sugar in a pestle and mortar
¼ teaspoon ground cardamom
25 g/1 oz (¼ cup) pistachios, roughly chopped

Photo on page 216.

This toffee brittle (known as *sohan-e-qom* in Farsi) originates from Qom, a holy city in Iran. Gently infused with fragrant saffron and cardamom, this crunchy toffee is perfect with a cup of strong coffee or hibiscus tea. I've also been known to crumble it over ice cream.

In Iran, it's usually made with wheat sprouts for a crunchy texture, but as they are hard to come by, I make mine with a little flour which cooks with the sugar, giving a toasty butteriness which I love.

Line a large baking sheet completely with parchment paper.

In a saucepan, combine the sugar, flour and 3 tablespoons of cold water. Clip a sugar thermometer onto the side of the saucepan. Heat for 5 minutes over medium heat, stirring occasionally, until the sugar is melted and dissolved.

Stir in the butter and syrup and bring to a boil. Boil until the temperature on the thermometer reaches 140°C/284°F, then immediately remove the pan from the heat. Stir in the ground saffron and cardamom. Take care as the mixture is extremely hot.

Using a rubber spatula, pour the molten liquid into the centre of the prepared baking sheet. Spread the sugar evenly over the parchment to a thickness of roughly 4 mm/⅙ inch. Immediately sprinkle with the pistachios, then place another sheet of parchment paper over the top. Using a rolling pin, press the nuts into the brittle. Leave to cool at room temperature for 1 hour, until set.

With clean hands, break up the brittle into shards, then transfer to an airtight container.

The brittle can be stored for up to 10 days.

COCONUT COOKIES

Makes about 15

For the cookies

125 g/4¼ oz (1⅓ cups) desiccated coconut
½ teaspoon ground cardamom
¼ teaspoon baking powder
Pinch of salt
½ teaspoon vanilla bean paste
6 tablespoons condensed milk
2 tablespoons coconut oil, melted
1 egg, beaten

For the lemon glaze

50 g/1¾ oz (⅓ cup) icing (confectioners') sugar
Juice of ½ lemon

Photo on page 217.

Known as 'The Tree of Life', coconut is prized for its economic, nutritional and cosmetic benefits.

Its sweet, buttery flavour also gets my vote. These pillowy cookies, not unlike macaroons, are a treat at any time of day.

Make the cookies. Preheat the oven to 170°C/340°F/Gas Mark 3. Line a large baking sheet with parchment paper.

In a large bowl, combine all the ingredients and mix well. Using a lightly greased melon baller or tablespoon measure, scoop rounds of the dough onto the prepared baking sheet, evenly spacing them 1 cm/½ inch apart. Bake for 15–18 minutes, until golden. Set aside to cool for 5 minutes. Using a cake slice, carefully transfer the cookies to a cooling rack to cool completely. They will still be crumbly at this point, so take your time.

Meanwhile, make the lemon glaze. Combine the icing (confectioners') sugar and enough lemon juice to form a thick, pourable glaze. Once the cookies have completely cooled, transfer to a plate and drizzle with the glaze.

The cookies will keep in an airtight container for up to 3 days.

ORANGE BLOSSOM APRICOTS WITH MASCARPONE

Serves 6

6 apricots, halved and pitted

3 tablespoons sugar

150 g/5½ oz mascarpone

1 tablespoon runny honey

1 teaspoon orange blossom water

40 g/1½ oz (½ cup) flaked (slivered) almonds or roughly chopped pistachios

1 tablespoon coriander seeds, roughly bashed in a pestle and mortar

Mulberry, Orange and Sesame Seed Brittle (page 228), to serve (optional)

Most Middle Eastern family meals conclude with fruit as they're so sweet and plentiful. In Lebanon, we always knew when soft stone fruit like apricots, peaches and plums were ready to be picked. The trees would be heavy with juicy, ripe fruit, and we could smell their heady aroma when walking past. This time of year was always a highlight for me.

Apricots and almonds work beautifully together, but you could use any stone fruit.

Preheat the grill (broiler) to the highest setting.

Arrange the apricots on a baking sheet, cut side up, and sprinkle the sugar over. Grill for 5–7 minutes, rotating them occasionally, until the cut sides are blistered and golden.

Meanwhile, in a bowl, combine the mascarpone, honey and orange blossom water and whisk until light and fluffy.

Transfer the apricots to a plate and set aside to cool for 10 minutes.

Gently toast the nuts and coriander seeds in a small frying pan or skillet, until golden and fragrant.

Place a heaped spoon of the mascarpone in each apricot hollow, then sprinkle over the toasted nuts. Serve with the brittle, if desired.

ORANGE AND ALMOND SYRUP CAKE

Serves 8

6 eggs, separated
200 g/7 oz (scant 1 cup) soft brown sugar
Grated zest of 2 oranges
Grated zest of 1 lemon
¼ teaspoon almond extract
225 g/8 oz (2⅔ cups) ground almonds
¼ teaspoon salt
Crème fraîche, to serve

For the syrup
Juice of 6 oranges
Juice of ½ lemon
250 g/9 oz (1 cup plus 2 tablespoons) runny honey
1 teaspoon orange blossom water

Impossibly light and syrupy at the same time, this citrus-y cake is perfect in the afternoon with a cup of tea or with a scoop of crème fraîche for a sophisticated evening dessert. Be sure to buy unwaxed oranges for this recipe: the zest, along with the juice, is a key ingredient.

Preheat the oven to 180°C/350°F/Gas Mark 4. Line a 23-cm/9-inch springform cake pan with parchment paper.

In a large mixing bowl, combine the egg yolks and sugar and beat until pale and fluffy. Add the citrus zests and almond extract and beat to combine. Stir in the ground almonds and mix well. Clean the whisk.

Cut the zested lemon in half. Rub the inside of a clean mixing bowl with a lemon half. Add the egg whites and beat until stiff peaks form. Fold the egg whites and salt into the almond mixture, until no white streaks are visible.

Pour the batter into the prepared pan. Bake on the middle rack for 40 minutes, or until a skewer inserted comes out clean.

Meanwhile, make the syrup. In a small saucepan, combine the citrus juices and bring to a boil. Reduce the heat to medium-low and simmer for 5 minutes, until reduced by a quarter. Add the honey and simmer for 8–10 minutes, until the mixture has thickened. Remove from the heat, then stir in the orange blossom water.

Prick the cake surface all over with a skewer. Pour over the syrup and leave to cool in the pan for 10 minutes. Release the cake, then transfer to a wire rack to cool completely.

Cut into wedges and serve with crème fraîche.

FUDGY SALTED DARK CHOCOLATE AND SESAME KISSES

Makes about 40 kisses (little cookies)

250 g/9 oz dark (bittersweet) chocolate (at least 70% cocoa solids), roughly chopped
1½ tablespoons butter
1½ tablespoons tahini
1 teaspoon vanilla bean paste
½ teaspoon salt
2 eggs
175 g/6 oz (¾ cup) soft dark brown sugar
60 g/2¼ oz (½ cup) buckwheat flour or dark (wholemeal) rye flour
2 tablespoons sesame seeds
Flaky sea salt, to finish

Bridging the gap between a fudgy brownie and a buttery cookie, these little kisses are a more-ish treat. They can also be prepared in advance: freeze the kisses on a tray after shaping them. When ready to serve, simply bake them from frozen and add another 1½ minutes to the cooking time.

In a heat-proof bowl, combine the chocolate, butter and tahini. Place the bowl over a saucepan of barely simmering water and melt the chocolate, ensuring the bottom of the bowl does not touch the water. Remove from the heat, then stir in the vanilla and salt.

In a large mixing bowl, beat the eggs with an electric whisk for 5 minutes, adding the sugar in 5 increments after each minute. The eggs should be pale in colour and voluminous. Stir in the melted chocolate mixture. Fold in the flour until incorporated. Cover and chill in the refrigerator for 30 minutes–2 hours.

Preheat the oven to 180°C/350°F/Gas Mark 4. Line 2 large baking sheets with parchment paper.

Take a tablespoon of the mixture and rub between clean palms to form a ball. Place on one of the lined baking sheets and sprinkle with a few sesame seeds and a small pinch of flaky salt.

Repeat with the remaining dough, seeds and salt. Bake in the oven for 6–7 minutes until the surfaces look cracked, but they are still soft in the middle. Leave to cool on the tray for 5 minutes before transferring to a rack to cool completely.

Store in an airtight container for up to 3 days.

DRINKS

L–R Sahlab (page 249), Frappe (page 244), Pomegranate Juice (page 248), Melon and Mint Sparkler (page 248).

CREAMY ALMOND SMOOTHIE

Serves 2

- 3 pieces mastic gum, crushed with ¼ teaspoon sugar in a pestle and mortar
- 1 ripe banana
- 60 g/2 oz (½ cup) blanched almonds
- ⅛ teaspoon salt
- 180 ml/6 fl oz (¾ cup) almond milk
- 1 tablespoon date syrup, plus extra to taste
- ½ teaspoon orange blossom water
- 2 handfuls of ice cubes
- Ground cinnamon, for sprinkling

Rich and refreshing, the creaminess of almonds is used here to full effect.

Mastic is a plant resin derived from trees, which has a pleasant piney flavour when ground. You can find mastic gum at Middle Eastern shops or online. If you're unable to find it, just add less date syrup.

Combine all the ingredients, except the cinnamon, in a blender and blend until smooth. Season to taste with more date syrup.

Pour into 2 long glasses. Sprinkle with the cinnamon and serve.

MELON AND YOGURT SMOOTHIE

Serves 2

- 1 cantaloupe (about 700 g/1 lb 9 oz), cut in half and seeded
- 150 g/5½ oz (scant ¾ cup) Greek yogurt
- Juice of 2 blood oranges (see Note)
- Small thumb-sized piece of fresh ginger, peeled and roughly chopped
- ½ teaspoon vanilla bean paste
- Pinch of salt
- Handful of ice cubes
- Date syrup or honey, to sweeten (optional)

Note

If you cannot find blood oranges, replace each with ½ orange and ½ lemon.

Rich and cooling, this is all I want for breakfast on a hot summer's day. When choosing melons, look for fruit that feels heavy for its size without any dark discolouration on the skin.

Place the melon, cut side down, on a chopping (cutting) board. Using a sharp knife, cut off the peel. Chop the melon into 3-cm/1¼-inch chunks, then place them in a blender with the remaining ingredients except the date syrup or honey. Add 3 tablespoons of water. Blend until smooth, then sweeten to taste with the date syrup or honey.

Pour into glasses, then serve.

The smoothie can be covered and stored in the refrigerator up to 6 hours.

LOVE TEA

Serves 2

12 saffron strands
2 tablespoons dried edible hibiscus flowers
1 tablespoon sugar or honey
Juice of ½ lemon

It's no great secret that Iranians love saffron – grown in the country, it's often regarded as the best in the world. In Persian culture, versions of this have been used to combat depression, anxiety and to act as an aphrodisiac.

I love the rich and tannic flavour of hibiscus, which is also the key ingredient for this tea's wonderful colour.

Place the saffron and hibiscus in a teapot and pour over 475 ml/16 fl oz (2 cups) of boiling water. Steep for at least 5 minutes.

Strain the liquid into a jug (pitcher). Stir in the sugar and lemon until the sugar is dissolved.

Pour into glasses and serve warm or cool.

FRAPPE

Serves 1

3 tablespoons espresso
100 ml/3½ fl oz (scant ½ cup) milk
1 teaspoon sugar
Handful of ice cubes

It's little wonder that iced coffees are so popular in the Middle East – coffee is one of the most popular reasons for meeting up socially (as many locals don't drink alcohol). This super simple *frappe* (blended iced coffee) can be made with Arabic coffee or flavoured syrups too, if you prefer.

Combine all the ingredients in a blender. Add 100 ml/3½ fl oz (scant ½ cup) water and blend until the ice is crushed and the frappe is thick and frothy. Pour into a tall glass and serve immediately.

Photo on page 240.

SWEET HAWAIJ COFFEE

Serves 2

100 ml/3½ fl oz (scant ½ cup) espresso
6 tablespoons milk or plant-based milk
½ teaspoon Sweet Hawaij (page 255)
½–1 teaspoon soft dark brown sugar

Pictured opposite.

***Hawaij* is a spice blend that originated in Yemen, of which there are both sweet and savoury versions (page 255). The first time I served this to a friend who had lived in the States, she said that it reminded her of a pumpkin spiced latte – but so much more delicious. Her words not mine.**

Combine all the ingredients in a small saucepan over medium heat, stirring continuously, until thoroughly warmed through. Pour into small cups and serve.

TAHINI-SPICED HOT CHOCOLATE

Serves 2

75 g/2¾ oz dark (bittersweet) chocolate (at least 70% cocoa solids), roughly chopped
3 tablespoons tahini
400 ml/14 fl oz (1⅔ cups) milk
2 teaspoons honey
1 teaspoon Sweet Hawaij (page 255)
Pinch of salt

If you've made tahini sauce, you'll know that tahini tends to thicken when mixed with other ingredients. (And if you haven't, you will after cooking through this book!) It reminds me of thick Spanish hot chocolate, made for dipping *churros* (Spanish donuts), although you're more likely to find me dipping a Lebanese donut (page 266) into mine.

Bring a saucepan of water to a gentle simmer over medium heat. In a heatproof bowl suspended over the pan, combine the chocolate and tahini. Ensure the bottom of the bowl does not touch the surface of the water. (If needed, drain out some of the water or use a different bowl.) Cook for 5 minutes, stirring occasionally, until the chocolate has completely melted.

Meanwhile, in a separate saucepan, combine the milk, honey, hawaij and salt. Whisk over low heat until the pan starts to steam. (Do not let it boil.) Using a rubber spatula, scrape the melted chocolate mixture into the pan and whisk to combine. Once the mixture comes to a near boil, pour into mugs and serve.

POMEGRANATE JUICE

Makes 650 ml/22 fl oz (2¾ cups)

4 pomegranates or 800 g/1 lb 12 oz (4½ cups) pomegranate seeds

Photo on page 241.

When choosing pomegranates, seek out fruits that are unblemished and feel heavy for their size (an indication of how much juice is inside). A word of advice: wear dark clothes or an apron when making this juice! The seeds tend to burst enthusiastically from the fruit, staining like red wine.

If using fresh pomegranates, prepare a large bowl of cold water. Using a serrated knife, cut the 'crown' off of each pomegranate. Score the skin into quarter wedges. Pull away each wedge of skin, then rub clean fingers over the pomegranate seeds to release them over the bowl of water. This helps to separate the seeds from any papery pith.

Use a slotted spoon to scoop out the pith floating on the surface, then discard. Drain the seeds, removing any lingering pith and transfer to a blender. Blend for a minute.

Strain the mixture through a fine-mesh sieve into a clean bowl. Using a rubber spatula, press down on the pulp to release as much of the juice as possible. When the pulp looks dry, decant the juice into a sterilised jar with a lid.

The juice can be stored in the refrigerator for up to 5 days.

MELON AND MINT SPARKLER

Serves 4

1 honeydew melon, cut in half and seeded
3 sprigs mint, leaves only, plus extra to garnish
1 teaspoon rosewater
Pinch of salt
Juice of ½ lime
475 ml/16 fl oz (2 cups) sparkling water
Lime slices (optional), to garnish

Photo on page 241.

I make this sparkler on the warmest days of the year. The 'ice cubes' made from frozen chunks of melon are cooling and less teeth-shattering than ice. A little salt is often added to Middle Eastern drinks to replace the salt lost from the body on a hot day and to intensify the fruity flavours.

Peel half the melon, then cut the flesh into 2-cm/¾-inch cubes. Arrange in an even layer on a parchment-lined baking sheet and place in the freezer for at least 2 hours, or overnight.

Using a spoon, scoop out the flesh from the unpeeled melon into a jug (pitcher). Add the mint, rosewater, salt and lime juice. Using the end of a rolling pin or a pestle, muddle the ingredients together. Strain through a fine-mesh sieve into a bowl, pressing down on the melon mixture to extract as much of the juice as possible. Transfer the bowl to the refrigerator.

Place a few frozen melon cubes into glasses, then divide the juice among the glasses. Top with sparkling water, then garnish with a sprig of mint or slice of lime.

SAHLAB

Serves 4

2 tablespoons sahlab powder
500 ml/17 fl oz (2 cups plus 1 tablespoon) milk
2 tablespoons honey, plus extra to taste

To garnish
½ teaspoon ground cinnamon
1 tablespoon golden raisins
1 teaspoon flaked (slivered) pistachios

Photo on page 240.

Thick and laced with gentle spicing, *sahlab* is my ultimate comfort food. Depending on where you are in the Levant, it can be consumed hot on a chilly day or cooled and set in bowls, adorned with cinnamon, nuts and jewels of dried fruit.

I serve it as a drink in this recipe, but it will set if cooled and transferred to the refrigerator for an hour or so. Feel free to experiment if the mood takes you.

Derived from orchard root, sahlab powder has a distinctly aromatic, floral scent and flavour. It is available at Middle Eastern shops or online.

Combine the sahlab powder and 4 tablespoons of water in a saucepan and bring to a boil over medium-high heat. Whisk continuously for 5 minutes, until the mixture thickens and becomes stretchy and sticky.

Remove from the heat and pour in the milk. Heat over the lowest heat and whisk in the honey. Cook gently for 15–20 minutes, whisking continuously, until slightly thickened and smooth. If it's lumpy, use an immersion blender to blend the mixture.

Pour into glasses. Top with cinnamon, golden raisins and pistachios.

SALTED YOGURT COOLER

Serves 2

200 g/7 oz (scant 1 cup) Greek yogurt
100 ml/3½ fl oz (scant ½ cup) sparkling water
½ teaspoon fine salt
1 teaspoon honey (optional)

Known as *ayran*, this is a popular Turkish drink, famed for its foamy surface. It's sour but incredibly refreshing. If the taste is not up your street, drizzle in a teaspoon of honey.

Place all the ingredients except the honey in a large jar. Screw the lid on tightly and shake vigorously for a minute.

Fill 2 glasses with ice, then pour the *ayran*. Drizzle in the honey, if using, and serve immediately.

SPICES, SAUCES & PRESERVES

L–R Mango Amba Sauce (page 259), Baharat (page 254). Chilli Oil (page 257).

ZA'ATAR

Makes 1 x (300-ml/10-fl oz) jar

- 4 tablespoons sesame seeds
- 6 tablespoons dried thyme
- 6 tablespoons sumac
- ½ teaspoon salt

Wild thyme, or *za'atar* in Arabic, grows wild in the mountains and hedgerows across the Levantine. And this herb is the star ingredient in this eponymous Levantine spice blend.

The dried thyme available in the West is different but similar enough. In some parts of the Middle East, you can buy the regally named 'royal red za'atar' in decorative jars, layered with desiccated coconut and pistachios. It is far too sweet for my tastes but well-worth seeking out in specialist shops if you're a za'atar fan.

While za'atar can be found on supermarket shelves across the UK these days, I encourage you to make it at home. It's easy to make and infinitely better than store-bought products.

Toast the sesame seeds in a dry frying pan or skillet over medium heat for 2–3 minutes, or until light golden.

In a food processor, combine the thyme, sumac and salt and grind until finely ground. Transfer to a bowl. Stir in the toasted sesame seeds.

Transfer to a clean 300-ml/10-fl oz jar. Cover and store at room temperature for up to 6 months.

BAHARAT

Makes 1 x (200-g/7-oz) jar

- 3 tablespoons black peppercorns
- 3 tablespoons cumin seeds
- 2 teaspoons cardamom seeds (see Note)
- 2 tablespoons coriander seeds
- ½ teaspoon cloves
- 3 tablespoons paprika
- 1 teaspoon ground cinnamon
- ¼ teaspoon grated nutmeg

The word *baharat* means 'spices' in Arabic, and this spice blend adds an earthy, highly aromatic depth to savoury dishes. I use it to marinate vegetables before roasting or to season my Baharat-Rubbed Mushroom Kebabs (page 80).

The removal of cardamom seeds from their pods may seem a little onerous, but it's essential to roast the seeds to coax out their aromatic oils and flavour. (Ground spices lose their potency over time.) If you're pressed for time, you can use ground cardamom but toast it first.

One by one, toast the whole spices in a dry frying pan or skillet over medium heat for 1–2 minutes. Stir them frequently to prevent them from burning. Transfer the toasted whole spices to a bowl.

Take the pan off the heat and add the paprika, cinnamon and nutmeg. Stir for 30 seconds until fragrant, then transfer to the bowl of whole spices.

Tip the mixture into a spice grinder or pestle and mortar and grind until finely ground.

Transfer to an airtight container and store at room temperature for up to 6 months.

Note

Crush the cardamom pods to release the seeds.

Photo on page 252.

DUKKAH

Makes 1 x (500-ml/17-fl oz) jar

100 g/3½ oz (generous ½ cup) hazelnuts
70 g/2½ oz (scant ½ cup) pistachios
2½ tablespoons cumin seeds
2½ tablespoons coriander seeds
2 tablespoons fennel seeds
2 tablespoons sesame seeds
1 teaspoon salt

Made from spices, nuts and seeds, this crunchy seasoning can be sprinkled over yogurt to serve alongside grilled vegetables or added to olive oil to make a delicious dip for pitta breads. I also sprinkle it over cooked vegetables, halloumi or tofu for a flavour boost.

Preheat the oven to 180°C/350°F/Gas Mark 4.

Spread out the hazelnuts and pistachios on 2 baking sheets. Toast in the oven for 6 minutes, until light golden and fragrant. Set aside.

When cool enough to handle, place the hazelnuts in the centre of a clean dish towel and cover. Rub the sides of the dish towel together to remove the skins. Transfer the hazelnuts and pistachios to a food processor.

Meanwhile, toast the seeds, one by one, in a frying pan or skillet over medium-high heat, until aromatic. Set aside 1 teaspoon from each batch of toasted seeds. Add the remaining seeds to the food processor, then pulse until it forms a coarse powder. Transfer the mixture to a bowl. Stir in the reserved seeds and salt.

Transfer to a sterilised 500-ml/17-fl oz jar. Cover and store at room temperature for up to a month.

SWEET HAWAIJ

Makes 2 tablespoons

8 cloves
½ stick cinnamon
1 tablespoon cardamom seeds (see Note, opposite)
½ teaspoon ground ginger
½ teaspoon ground mace

This intriguing and aromatic spice blend can be stirred into milky coffees or used in sweet bakes, in lieu of mixed spice or cinnamon.

Hawaij **(meaning 'mixture' in Arabic) can also be savoury by blending cumin, black pepper, turmeric and cardamom. It's often used to marinate savoury dishes.**

Toast the cloves, cinnamon and cardamom seeds in a frying pan or skillet over medium heat for 4–5 minutes, until fragrant. (Take care not to burn.) Remove from the heat, then stir in the ginger and mace. Transfer to a plate to cool immediately.

Transfer to a spice grinder or pestle and mortar and grind until finely ground.

Transfer to an airtight jar and store at room temperature for up to 3 months.

POMEGRANATE MOLASSES

Makes 1 x (200-ml/7-fl oz) bottle or jar

1 quantity Pomegranate Juice (page 248)
2 tablespoons sugar
Juice of ½ lemon

Yes, you can buy pomegranate molasses at most corner shops these days. But like most things in life, it tastes better homemade. Be sure to keep an eye on the pan while the liquid reduces – it can catch and burn if you turn your back for too long.

Combine all the ingredients in a saucepan. Cook over low heat for 5 minutes, stirring regularly, until the sugar is dissolved.

Increase the heat to medium-high and bring to a boil. Reduce the heat to medium and gently simmer for 40–45 minutes, until reduced by half and deep purple. Check every now and then that it's not boiling rapidly.

Pour the molasses into a sterilised 200-ml/7-fl oz bottle, then set aside to cool, uncovered.

Pomegranate molasses can be covered and stored in the refrigerator for up to 6 months.

ROSE HARISSA

Makes 1 x (200-ml/7-fl oz) jar

100 ml/3½ fl oz (scant ½ cup) extra-virgin olive oil, plus extra for greasing
3 red chillies, seeded and halved lengthwise
2 red peppers, seeded and quartered
3 garlic cloves
½ teaspoon salt, plus extra
25 edible dried rose petals
1 tablespoon tomato purée (paste)
½ teaspoon rosewater

With its subtle smokiness and lingering heat, this flavourful paste tastes of the time and care taken to make it. Harissa can be made without rose petals, but I find the spiciness too harsh in these instances. Here, the subtle floral note lends a depth of flavour to savoury dishes and marinades.

I like to use it in Harissa and Lime Aubergines with Crushed Chickpeas (page 174) or as a topping for fried egg on toast.

Preheat the oven to 120°C/250°F/Gas Mark ½. Lightly grease a roasting pan.

Arrange the chillies and peppers, cut side down, on the prepared roasting pan. Nestle the garlic cloves around the peppers and drizzle over 2 tablespoons of the oil. Season with salt. Roast for 90 minutes, or until the peppers are soft and their skins are slightly wrinkled. Remove them from the oven and discard any stalks.

Transfer the mixture to a food processor. Add three-quarters of the remaining oil, the rose petals, tomato purée (paste) and rosewater and process until a rough paste forms.

Transfer the mixture to a saucepan and add the salt. Cook over low heat for 2 hours, stirring occasionally, until it is a dark red paste with a deep, rich flavour.

Transfer to a sterilised 200-ml/7-fl oz jar. Top with the remaining oil and store in the refrigerator for up to 3 weeks.

ZHUG

Makes about 150 ml/5 fl oz (⅔ cup)

Bunch of coriander (cilantro) (about 30 g/1 oz)
Bunch of parsley (about 30 g/1 oz)
1 teaspoon cumin seeds, toasted and coarsely ground
⅛ teaspoon ground cardamom
3 garlic cloves
3 mild green chillies, seeded and roughly chopped
3 tablespoons extra-virgin olive oil
Juice of ½ lemon, plus extra
¼ teaspoon sugar, plus extra
salt (optional)

Packed with fresh vibrant herbs and a distinctive thread of aromatic chilli, zhug has just enough heat to create zing in a dish without completely overpowering the other flavours. Use it to enliven roasted potatoes, vegetable soup, marinated vegetables and tofu or as an herbaceous dipping sauce for flatbreads with grassy olive oil.

Dry the coriander and parsley in a salad spinner. Transfer them, with the stems, to a food processor. Add the remaining ingredients and blitz until smooth. Season to taste with more sugar, lemon juice and/or salt. Transfer to a jar.

Zhug can be covered and stored in the refrigerator for up to a week.

CHILLI OIL

Makes 1 x (300-ml/10-fl oz) jar

250 ml/8 fl oz (1 cup) extra-virgin olive oil
10 garlic cloves, finely chopped
50 g/1¾ oz (scant ½ cup) walnuts, finely chopped
2 tablespoons chilli flakes
1 teaspoon salt

Photo on page 253.

This deeply savoury condiment is perfect on everything from pizzas to creamy chickpea stews. Use the best olive oil and freshest garlic you can find as they will have a massive impact on the taste.

Heat the oil in a saucepan over medium heat for 2 minutes. Add the remaining ingredients and sauté until they begin to sizzle. Reduce the heat to medium-low and sauté for 5 minutes, until the mixture no longer smells like bananas skins (trust me!). Be sure not to burn the garlic or walnuts as it will make the oil bitter. If necessary, reduce the heat.

Transfer the oil to a sterilised 300-ml/10-fl oz jar. Leave to cool, then cover and set aside for 1 week before use.

The chilli oil can be stored in the refrigerator for up to 6 months.

ARABIC GARLIC SAUCE

Makes about 550 ml/18 fl oz (2½ cups)

2 heads garlic, cloves separated and peeled

1½ teaspoons salt

Juice of 1½ lemons

475 ml/16 fl oz (2 cups) vegetable or rapeseed (canola) oil

40 ml/1½ fl oz (3 tablespoons) extra-virgin olive oil

In the Middle East, Arabic garlic sauce, or *toum*, can be either a thin sauce for drizzling or a thick condiment. Imagine a super-charged garlic mayonnaise without the egg.

The garlic is first blended into a paste to release its chemicals and help emulsify the sauce after it's combined with the liquid ingredients. Alternate amounts of oil and lemon juice to stabilise everything, preventing the sauce from splitting.

Use the garlic sauce as you would do a mayonnaise or on Za'atar Fries (page 23), kebabs, falafel and burgers.

Combine the garlic cloves and salt in a food processor. Process over high speed for 3 minutes, occasionally scraping down the sides, until smooth. Add 1 teaspoon lemon juice and blend until smooth and glossy.

With the food processor running on low speed, slowly pour in 100 ml/3½ fl oz (scant ½ cup) of the oil. Add another 1 teaspoon of lemon juice and 100 ml/3½ fl oz (scant ½ cup) of the vegetable oil in a very slow stream. (This will prevent the mixture from breaking.) Alternate amounts of oil and lemon juice, until both are completely used up. Slowly pour in the olive oil until the mixture is smooth, thick and fluffy. If it splits, see note left.

Leftover sauce can be covered and stored in an airtight container in the refrigerator for up to 1 month.

Note

If the sauce splits, remove three-quarters of the mixture from the bowl. Add an egg white to the remaining quarter and blend to combine. Slowly pour in the remaining mixture until the sauce has thickened. Leftover mixture can be stored for up to 4 days.

GARLIC TAHINI SAUCE

Makes 1 x (250-ml/8-fl oz) jar

3 garlic cloves, roughly chopped

100 ml/3½ fl oz (scant ½ cup) tahini, well stirred

Juice of 1 lemon (about 2½ tablespoons)

¼ teaspoon salt

½ teaspoon date syrup, honey or sugar (optional)

I prepare a big jar of this and store it in the refrigerator until needed. It's great for drizzling over grain salads, falafel, grilled vegetables and crispy potatoes.

This creamy, garlicky condiment is ubiquitous at Levantine street food stalls, and with good reason. It lifts crispy, deep-fried snacks and balances out the bold flavours in burgers and shawarmas.

Add all the ingredients, except the date syrup, if using, to a food processor. Blitz to combine. With the motor still running, slowly pour in 100 ml/3½ fl oz (scant ½ cup) cold water and blend until smooth. Taste and add sweetener, if using.

Transfer the sauce to a sterilised 250-ml/8-fl oz jar. The sauce can be covered and stored in the refrigerator for up to a month.

MANGO AMBA SAUCE

Makes 3 x (300-ml/10-fl oz) jars

- 3 unripe, green mangoes, peeled with a vegetable peeler
- 1 tablespoon salt
- 2 tablespoons vegetable or rapeseed (canola) oil
- 3 garlic cloves, minced
- 1 mild red chilli, seeded and finely chopped
- 1 teaspoon yellow mustard seeds
- 1 teaspoon fenugreek seeds
- 1 teaspoon cumin seeds
- 1 teaspoon ground coriander
- 150 g/5½ oz (⅔ cup) dark brown sugar
- ¼ teaspoon ground cinnamon
- 120 ml/4 fl oz (½ cup) white wine vinegar
- 1 tablespoon sumac

Photo on page 252.

While this gently spiced condiment has Indian-Jewish origins, it is commonly served in Iraq and Israel – as a flavourful sauce option at falafel stands or alongside Spiced Tomato and Bean Samosas (page 34). I don't know why it hasn't caught on in the same way as mango chutney, but perhaps time will change that.

This perky hot sauce is relatively straightforward to make – just be sure to salt the mangoes for at least 24 hours first.

Cut the mangoes into 1-cm/½-inch cubes, discarding the pith. This should make about 750 g/1 lb 10 oz mango flesh.

Combine the mango and salt in a non-reactive bowl and toss well. Cover and refrigerate for 24–72 hours.

Heat the oil in a saucepan over medium heat. Add the garlic and chilli and sauté for 3 minutes, until softened but not coloured. Add the spices and sauté for a minute until aromatic. Stir in the sugar, cinnamon and mango with its curing liquid. Pour in the vinegar, 250 ml/8 oz (1 cup) water and sumac and cover with a lid. Simmer for 5 minutes, until the mango is tender.

Blend with an immersion blender, then transfer to a sterilised jar and cover. Serve with falafel, samosas or flatbreads with cheese.

The sauce can be stored in the refrigerator for up to a month.

SPICED PRESERVED LIMES

Makes 1 x (1-litre/34-fl oz) jar

1 mild green chilli, cut in half and seeded
½ teaspoon coriander seeds
½ teaspoon fennel seeds
6 unwaxed limes, plus 2 extra to juice
Fine salt, for packing
6 bay leaves

It's important that you use unwaxed limes for this recipe, because you'll be eating the skin and pith. (Not the juicy flesh inside, which will be discarded as it's too salty to eat.) Most citrus sold in the UK is waxed to prolong its shelf life and to make the fruit shiny and appealing yet inedible. Unwaxed fruit will be labelled as such – if you can't find it, leave the waxed limes in a bowl of hot water for 10 minutes, then use a vegetable scrubbing brush to rub away the wax.

Place the chilli, coriander and fennel seeds in a sterilised 1-litre/34-fl oz jar.

Place a lime on a chopping (cutting) board and cut 2 mm/¹⁄₁₆ inch from the bottom, so it stands upright on the chopping board. Cut an 'x' on the top (pointed) end, stopping short about three-quarters of the way down and leaving the fruit intact. Squeeze the base to push open the top of the lime. Hold the lime over the jar, then sprinkle a teaspoon of the salt into the crevices. Place the salted lime into the jar, pushing it down with your fist to pack the lime. Push the bay leaves into the jar. Repeat with 5 more limes, sprinkling with 1 teaspoon salt after each addition. Cover the jar and store in a cool place.

The next day, push down on the limes with your fist again to compact the limes and release their juices. On day 3, repeat until the limey brine created by the salt and limes completely covers the fruit. If the limes are not completely submerged, squeeze over the juice of 1–2 more limes, until covered. Set aside to ferment for 1 month.

Preserved limes can be stored in the refrigerator for up to 6 months.

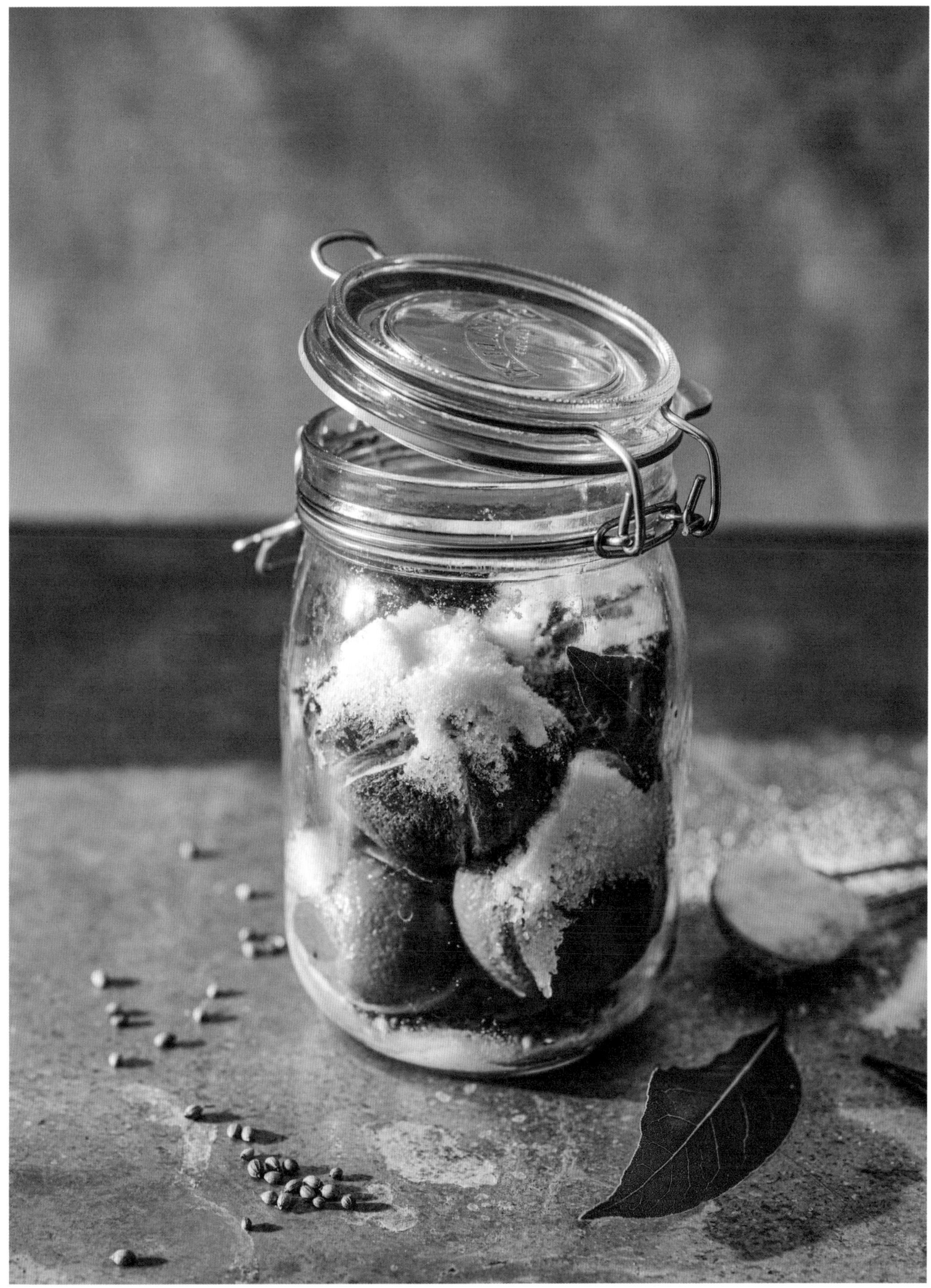

INDEX

Page numbers in *italics* refer to illustrations

A

akawi cheese with honey 30, *31*
Aleppo pepper sauce *48*, 49
almond milk: creamy almond smoothie *242*, 243
almonds
- creamy almond smoothie *242*, 243
- favourite baklava 218, *219*
- orange and almond syrup cake 234, *235*
- orange blossom apricots with mascarpone 232, *233*
- pepper and almond salsa 151–2, *153*
- spiced carrot salad 74, *156*

apples: fermented red onions 64
apricots: orange blossom apricots with mascarpone 232, *233*
Arabic garlic sauce 258
arayes, squash and walnut *79*, 83
aubergines (eggplants)
- aubergine and tomato mezze 158, *159*
- aubergine and yogurt mezze 18, *19*
- aubergine fries 14, *15*
- dukkah-crusted halloumi skewers *168*, 169
- harissa and lime aubergines with crushed chickpeas 174, *175*
- sweet and sour aubergine sliders 92, *93*

B

Baharat 252, 254
- Baharat-rubbed mushroom kebabs 80, *81*
- Baharat-spiced *vada pav* with date and tamarind chutney 84, *85*
- Egyptian *koshari* 136, *137*

baklava
- favourite baklava 218, *219*
- savoury baklava pie 184, *185*

bananas: creamy almond smoothie *242*, 243
barberries: sumac and barberry herb salad 66, *67*
basil: spiced herb sauce 80, *81*
beans
- beetroot koftes *96*, 105
- olive oil beans with tomatoes, garlic and herbs *140*, 141
- popped beans with pickled red onion and garlic labneh 144, *145*
- spiced tomato and bean samosas 34
- white bean *pkaila* with harissa squash 186, *187*
- *see also individual types of bean*

beetroot (beets)
- beetroot and feta fritters with cumin-dill yogurt 164, *165*
- beetroot koftes *96*, 105
- beetroot *muhammara* *12*, 16, *17*
- fermented beetroot and turnips *57*, 65
- hummus and pickled vegetable wrap *78*, 82

beignets, parsnip and cumin *28*, 44
biscuits
- coconut cookies *217*, 231
- fudgy salted dark chocolate and sesame kisses 236, *237*
- grilled peaches and toasted sesame shortbread 220, *221*

black-eyed beans (peas): Syrian black-eyed beans and greens 142, *143*
black limes
- black lime and herb tofu 50, *51*
- tofu *gondi* dumplings with black lime in tomato sauce 188, *189*

borani: spinach *borani* with walnuts 172
braised cardamom greens and yogurt *156*, 160, *161*
braised chickpeas with sumac greens 118, *119*
braised runner beans with tomato and cardamom *157*, 179
bread
- Baharat-spiced *vada pav* with date and tamarind chutney 84, *85*
- garlic and walnut dip *12*, 16, *17*
- spiced carrot and chickpea falafel burgers *86*, 87
- za'atar tomato toast 110, *111*

breads 192–213
- herb and feta flatbreads 196
- layered garlic and sesame flatbread 200, *201*
- Lebanese flatbread 198, *199*
- Lebanese ring bread *204*, 205
- *manakish* 206, *207*
- spinach *kulcha* *194*, 208
- spring onion and herb roti *210*, 211
- taboon bread *196*, 209
- Turkish sesame bread 197
- za'atar garlic bread 212, *213*
- za'atar parathas 202, *203*

breakfast buns: little rice breakfast buns with harissa eggs 100, *101*
brittle
- mulberry, orange and sesame seed brittle 228
- Persian toffee brittle *216*, 230

broth: spiced chickpeas in broth with whipped tahini yogurt *116*, 117
brunch 94–111
buckwheat (soba) noodles: za'atar cucumber noodle salad 72, *73*
bulgur wheat
- bulgur *mujadara* with nutty red pepper salsa 134, *135*
- celebration pie *190*, 191

burger buns
- Baharat-spiced *vada pav* with date and tamarind chutney 84, *85*
- spiced carrot and chickpea falafel burgers *86*, 87
- sweet and sour aubergine sliders 92, *93*

burgers, spiced carrot and chickpea falafel *86*, 87
butter
- grilled corn on the cob with sumac butter *163*
- saffron-butter sauce 170, *171*

butter (lima) beans
- beetroot koftes *96*, 105
- olive oil beans with tomatoes, garlic and herbs *140*, 141
- popped beans with pickled red onion and garlic labneh 144, *145*

butternut squash: squash and walnut *arayes* *79*, 83

C

cabbage
- charred summer cabbage with pomegranate molasses and walnuts *162*, 163
- fermented red cabbage *62*, 63
- Lebanese cabbage salad 70, *71*
- red cabbage shawarma *88*, 89
- sumac greens 118, *119*
- sweet and sour aubergine sliders 92, *93*

cake, orange and almond syrup 234, *235*
cake, savoury: herb and couscous cake with pepper and almond salsa 151–2, *153*
cannellini beans
- beetroot koftes *96*, 105
- olive oil beans with tomatoes, garlic and herbs *140*, 141
- popped beans with pickled red onion and garlic labneh 144, *145*
- spiced tomato and bean samosas 34

caramel
- caramelised onions 134, *135*
- spiced caramelised onion and tofu pastries *29*, 45

cardamom seeds
- Baharat *252*, 254

braised cardamom greens and yogurt *156*, 160, *161*
braised runner beans with tomato and cardamom *157*, 179
sweet *hawaij* 255
carrots
roasted carrot mezze *13*, 180, *181*
spiced carrot and chickpea falafel burgers *86*, 87
spiced carrot salad 74, *156*
spiced lentil and pine nut curry *47*, 128
cauliflower
cauliflower *musakhan* 166, *167*
cumin squash stew with cauliflower and pine nut crumble *114*, 129
red lentil soup with spiced cauliflower 124, *125*
celebration pie *190*, 191
charred summer cabbage with pomegranate molasses and walnuts *162*, 163
cheese
akawi cheese with honey 30, *31*
Baharat-rubbed mushroom kebabs 80, *81*
beetroot and feta fritters with cumin-dill yogurt 164, *165*
braised chickpeas with sumac greens 118, *119*
cheese and herb pastries 32, *33*
cheesy sweetcorn nuggets *36*, 37
cheesy za'atar swirls 38, *39*
dukkah-crusted halloumi skewers *168*, 169
fatayer with spinach and chickpeas 35, *36*
halloumi and za'atar spring rolls 42, *43*
herb and couscous cake with pepper and almond salsa 151–2, *153*
herb and feta flatbreads 196
kale and cheese kataifi bakes *40*, 41
knafeh 222, *223*
manakish 206, *207*
parsnip and cumin beignets 44
ricotta balls with preserved lemon and Aleppo pepper *48*, 49
roasted courgette salad with halloumi and mint 182, *183*
savoury baklava pie 184, *185*
sesame halloumi fries with chilli yogurt 24, *25*
squash and walnut *arayes* *79*, 83
sumac and barberry herb salad 66, *67*
sweet and sour aubergine sliders 92, *93*
watermelon and feta salad 70, *71*
see also cream cheese; mascarpone; ricotta
chickpeas
braised chickpeas with sumac greens 118, *119*
Egyptian *koshari* 136, *137*
fatayer with spinach and chickpeas 35, *36*
harissa and lime aubergines with crushed chickpeas 174, *175*
Lebanese chickpea and garlic stew with quick pickled radishes *115*, 122
pea and za'atar falafel 148, *149*
quick falafel 146, *147*
spiced carrot and chickpea falafel burgers *86*, 87
spiced chickpeas in broth with whipped tahini yogurt *116*, 117
spicy roasted chickpeas 14, *15*
chillies
chilli oil *253*, 257
chilli yogurt 24, *25*
rose harissa 256
semolina porridge with charred chilli corn 102, *103*
zhug 257
chocolate
fudgy salted dark chocolate and sesame kisses 236, *237*
tahini-spiced hot chocolate 246
chutney, date and tamarind 202
cloves: sweet *hawaij* 255
coconut
coconut cookies *217*, 231
little rice breakfast buns with harissa eggs 100, *101*
sweet porridge 104
coconut milk: little rice breakfast buns with harissa eggs 100, *101*
coffee
frappe *240*, 244
no-churn tahini-espresso ice cream 228, *229*
sweet *hawaij* coffee 246, *247*
condensed milk
coconut cookies *217*, 231
no-churn tahini-espresso ice cream 228, *229*
sweet porridge 104
cookies
coconut cookies *217*, 231
fudgy salted dark chocolate and sesame kisses 236, *237*
cooler, salted yogurt 249
coriander (cilantro)
black lime and herb tofu 50, *51*
braised cardamom greens and yogurt *156*, 160, *161*
cheese and herb pastries 32, *33*
freekeh tabbouleh *138*, 139
herb and couscous cake with pepper and almond salsa 151–2, *153*
herb and feta flatbreads 196
herby yogurt 174, *175*
olive oil beans with tomatoes, garlic and herbs *140*, 141
spiced herb sauce 80, *81*
white bean *pkaila* with harissa squash 186, *187*
zhug 257
coriander seeds
Baharat *252*, 254
dukkah 255
corn
grilled corn on the cob with sumac butter *163*
semolina porridge with charred chilli corn 102, *103*
courgettes (zucchini)
celebration pie *190*, 191
courgette and pitta salad 58, *59*
roasted courgette salad with halloumi and mint 182, *183*
couscous
herb and couscous cake with pepper and almond salsa 151–2, *153*
Syrian black-eyed beans and greens 142, *143*
cream: no-churn tahini-espresso ice cream 228, *229*
cream cheese
cheesy sweetcorn nuggets *36*, 37
ka'ek egg sandwich 82
creamy almond smoothie *242*, 243
crisps: polenta crisps with herby olive salsa *20*, 21
crumble, cumin squash stew with cauliflower and pine nut *114*, 129
cucumber
cucumber salad 146, *147*
fresh and crunchy fattoush 60, *61*
shepherd's salad *73*, 75
za'atar cucumber noodle salad 72, *73*
cumin
Baharat *252*, 254
cumin-dill yogurt 164, *165*
cumin squash stew with cauliflower and pine nut crumble *114*, 129
dukkah 255
parsnip and cumin beignets *28*, 44
spicy roasted chickpeas 14, *15*
curry, spiced lentil and pine nut *47*, 128

D

dairy-free
Arabic garlic sauce 258
Baharat *252*, 254
baked spicy potatoes *177*, 178
beetroot koftes *96*, 105
black lime and herb tofu 50, *51*
braised runner beans with tomato and cardamom *157*, 179
bulgur *mujadara* with nutty red pepper salsa 134, *135*
chickpea pancakes 46, *47*
chilli oil *253*, 257
creamy almond smoothie *242*, 243
cumin squash stew with cauliflower and pine nut crumble *114*, 129
dukkah 255
fermented beetroot and turnips 65
fermented red cabbage *62*, 63
fermented red onions *56*, 64
freekeh tabbouleh *138*, 139
fresh and crunchy fattoush 60, *61*
garlic and walnut dip *12*, 16, *17*
garlic tahini sauce 258
hummus and pickled vegetable wrap *78*, 82
layered garlic and sesame flatbread 200, *201*
Lebanese cabbage salad 70, *71*
Lebanese flatbread 198, *199*
Lebanese herb omelette *98*, 99
lemon and honey potatoes 176, *177*
lime and herb baked rice *132*, 139
little rice breakfast buns with harissa eggs 100, *101*
love tea 244, *245*
manakish 206, *207*
mango amba sauce 259
melon and mint sparkler *241*, 248
molokhia stew 120, *121*
mulberry, orange and sesame seed brittle 228
pea and za'atar falafel 148, *149*
polenta crisps with herby olive salsa *20*, 21
pomegranate juice *241*, 248
pomegranate molasses 256
quick falafel 146, *147*
red lentil soup with spiced cauliflower 124, *125*
rose harissa 256
shepherd's salad *73*, 75
spiced carrot and chickpea falafel burgers *86*, 87
spiced carrot salad 74, *156*
spiced lentil and pine nut curry *47*, 128
spiced preserved limes 260, *261*
spiced tomato and bean samosas 34
spicy roasted chickpeas 14, *15*
summer vegetable grain salad *135*, 150
sweet *hawaij* 255
Syrian black-eyed beans and greens 142, *143*
taboon bread *196*, 209
tofu *gondi* dumplings with black lime in tomato sauce 188, *189*
tomato and pomegranate salad *67*, 74
Turkish sesame bread 197
white bean *pkaila* with harissa squash 186, *187*
za'atar 254
za'atar cucumber noodle salad 72, *73*
za'atar fries *13*, *22*, 23
za'atar tomato toast 110, *111*
zhug 257
date and tamarind chutney 202
Baharat-spiced *vada pav* with date and tamarind chutney 84, *85*
desserts 214–37
dill
black lime and herb tofu 50, *51*
braised cardamom greens and yogurt *156*, 160, *161*
cheese and herb pastries 32, *33*
cumin-dill yogurt 164, *165*
freekeh tabbouleh *138*, 139
herb and couscous cake with pepper and almond salsa 151–2, *153*
herb and feta flatbreads 196
herby yogurt 174, *175*
sumac and barberry herb salad 66, *67*
dips
beetroot *muhammara* *12*, 16, *17*
garlic and walnut dip *12*, 16, *17*
donut balls, little 226, *227*
dressing, tahini 72, *73*
drinks 238–49
creamy almond smoothie *242*, 243
frappe *240*, 244
love tea 244, *245*
melon and mint sparkler *241*, 248
melon and yogurt smoothie *242*, 243
pomegranate juice *241*, 248
sahlab *240*, 249
salted yogurt cooler 249
sweet *hawaij* coffee 246, *247*
tahini-spiced hot chocolate 246, *247*
dukkah 255
dukkah-crusted halloumi skewers *168*, 169
dumplings: tofu *gondi* dumplings with black lime in tomato sauce 188, *189*

E

eggs
ka'ek egg sandwich 82
Lebanese herb omelette *98*, 99
little rice breakfast buns with harissa eggs 100, *101*
orange and almond syrup cake 234, *235*
spiced scrambled eggs 106, *107*
Egyptian *koshari* 136, *137*
espresso
frappe *240*, 244
no-churn tahini-espresso ice cream 228, *229*
sweet *hawaij* coffee 246, *247*

F

falafels
pea and za'atar falafel 148, *149*
quick falafel 146, *147*
spiced carrot and chickpea falafel burgers *86*, 87
fatayer with spinach and chickpeas 35, *36*
fattoush, fresh and crunchy 60, *61*
favourite baklava 218, *219*
fennel: summer vegetable grain salad *135*, 150
fennel seeds: dukkah 255
fermented beetroot (beets)
hummus and pickled vegetable wrap *78*, 82
fermented beetroot and turnip *57*, 65
fermented red cabbage *62*, 63
fermented red onions 56, 64
black lime and herb tofu 50, *51*
feta
beetroot and feta fritters with cumin-dill yogurt 164, *165*
fatayer with spinach and chickpeas 35, *36*
herb and couscous cake with pepper and almond salsa 151–2, *153*
herb and feta flatbreads 196
kale and cheese kataifi bakes *40*, 41
savoury baklava pie 184, *185*

sumac and barberry herb salad 66, *67*
watermelon and feta salad 70, *71*
filo (phyllo) pastry
celebration pie *190*, 191
cheese and herb pastries 32, *33*
favourite baklava 218, *219*
savoury baklava pie 184, *185*
spiced tomato and bean samosas 34
five ingredients or less
Arabic garlic sauce 258
chilli oil *253*, 257
fermented red cabbage *62*, 63
fermented red onions *56*, 64
frappe *240*, 244
garlic tahini sauce 258
Lebanese flatbread 198, *199*
love tea 244, *245*
manakish 206, *207*
pomegranate juice *241*, 248
pomegranate molasses 256
salted yogurt cooler 249
sweet *hawaij* 255
sweet *hawaij* coffee 246, *247*
taboon bread *196*, 209
za'atar 254
za'atar fries *13*, *22*, 23
flatbreads
Baharat-spiced *vada pav* with date and tamarind chutney 84, *85*
herb and feta flatbreads 196
layered garlic and sesame flatbread 200, *201*
Lebanese flatbread 198, *199*
manakish 206, *207*
red cabbage shawarma *88*, 89
spinach *kulcha* *194*, 208
spring onion and herb roti *210*, 211
squash and walnut *arayes* *79*, 83
taboon bread *196*, 209
yogurt-marinated tofu shawarma 90, *91*
za'atar parathas 202, *203*
four seasons frozen labneh yogurt *224*, 225
frappe *240*, 244
freekeh
celebration pie *190*, 191
freekeh tabbouleh *138*, 139
summer vegetable grain salad *135*, 150
fresh and crunchy fattoush 60, *61*
fries
aubergine fries 14, *15*
sesame halloumi fries with chilli yogurt 24, *25*
za'atar fries *13*, *22*, 23
fritters: beetroot and feta fritters with cumin-dill yogurt 164, *165*
fruit
four seasons frozen labneh yogurt *224*, 225
see also individual types of fruit
fudgy salted dark chocolate and sesame kisses 236, *237*

G

garlic
Arabic garlic sauce 258
braised chickpeas with sumac greens 118, *119*
braised runner beans with tomato and cardamom *157*, 179
chilli oil *253*, 257
garlic and walnut dip *12*, 16, *17*
garlic labneh 144, *145*
garlic tahini sauce 258
garlic yogurt 44
layered garlic and sesame flatbread 200, *201*
Lebanese chickpea and garlic stew with quick pickled radishes *115*, 122
lentil soup with tamarind and greens 123, *133*
molokhia stew 120, *121*
olive oil beans with tomatoes, garlic and herbs *140*, 141
spiced chickpeas in broth with whipped tahini yogurt *116*, 117
yogurt-marinated tofu shawarma 90, *91*
za'atar garlic bread 212, *213*
gluten-free
Arabic garlic sauce 258
aubergine and tomato mezze 158, *159*
aubergine and yogurt mezze 18, *19*
aubergine fries 14, *15*
Baharat *252*, 254
baked spicy potatoes *177*, 178
beetroot *muhammara* *12*, 16, *17*
black lime and herb tofu 50, *51*
braised cardamom greens and yogurt *156*, 160, *161*
braised chickpeas with sumac greens 118, *119*
braised runner beans with tomato and cardamom *157*, 179
chickpea pancakes 46, *47*
chilli oil *253*, 257
coconut cookies *217*, 231
creamy almond smoothie *242*, 243
cumin squash stew with cauliflower and pine nut crumble *114*, 129
dukkah 255
fermented beetroot and turnips 65
fermented red cabbage *62*, 63
fermented red onions *56*, 64
four seasons frozen labneh yogurt *224*, 225
frappe *240*, 244
fudgy salted dark chocolate and sesame kisses 236, *237*
garlic tahini sauce 258
golden pumpkin with saffron-butter sauce 170, *171*
Lebanese cabbage salad 70, *71*
Lebanese chickpea and garlic stew with quick pickled radishes *115*, 122
lentil soup with tamarind and greens 123, *133*
lime and herb baked rice *132*, 139
little rice breakfast buns with harissa eggs 100, *101*
love tea 244, *245*
mango amba sauce 259
melon and mint sparkler *241*, 248
melon and yogurt smoothie *242*, 243
mint and preserved lime labneh 52, *53*
molokhia stew 120, *121*
mulberry, orange and sesame seed brittle 228
no-churn tahini-espresso ice cream 228, *229*
orange and almond syrup cake 234, *235*
orange blossom apricots with mascarpone 232, *233*
pomegranate juice *241*, 248
pomegranate molasses 256
red lentil soup with spiced cauliflower 124, *125*
roasted courgette salad with halloumi and mint 182, *183*
rose harissa 256
sahlab *240*, 249
salted yogurt cooler 249
shepherd's salad *73*, 75
smoky sumac onion salad 68, *69*
spiced carrot salad 74, *156*
spiced chickpeas in broth with whipped tahini yogurt *116*, 117
spiced lentil and pine nut curry *47*, 128
spiced preserved limes 260, *261*
spicy roasted chickpeas 14, *15*
spinach *borani* with walnuts 172

sumac and barberry herb salad 66, *67*
sweet *hawaij* 255
sweet *hawaij* coffee 246, *247*
tahini-spiced hot chocolate 246
tomato and pomegranate salad *67*, 74
watermelon and feta salad 70, *71*
white bean *pkaila* with harissa squash 186, *187*
za'atar 254
za'atar cucumber noodle salad 72, *73*
za'atar fries *13*, *22*, 23
zhug 257
goat's cheese: cheese and herb pastries 32, *33*
golden pumpkin with saffron-butter sauce 170, *171*
gondi dumplings: tofu *gondi* dumplings with black lime in tomato sauce 188, *189*
grains: summer vegetable grain salad *135*, 150
gram flour
Baharat-spiced *vada pav* with date and tamarind chutney 84, *85*
chickpea pancakes 46, *47*
greens
braised cardamom greens and yogurt *156*, 160, *161*
braised chickpeas with sumac greens 118, *119*
lentil soup with tamarind and greens 123, *133*
Syrian black-eyed beans and greens 142, *143*

H

halloumi
Baharat-rubbed mushroom kebabs 80, *81*
cheesy za'atar swirls 38, *39*
dukkah-crusted halloumi skewers *168*, 169
halloumi and za'atar spring rolls 42, *43*
kale and cheese kataifi bakes *40*, 41
manakish 206, *207*
parsnip and cumin beignets 44
roasted courgette salad with halloumi and mint 182, *183*
sesame halloumi fries with chilli yogurt 24, *25*
squash and walnut *arayes* 79, 83
sweet and sour aubergine sliders 92, *93*
harissa
harissa and lime aubergines with crushed chickpeas 174, *175*
little rice breakfast buns with harissa eggs 100, *101*
rose harissa 256
white bean *pkaila* with harissa squash 186, *187*
hawaij
sweet *hawaij* 255
sweet *hawaij* coffee 246, *247*
hazelnuts: dukkah 255
herbs
black lime and herb tofu 50, *51*
cheese and herb pastries 32, *33*
freekeh tabbouleh *138*, 139
herb and couscous cake with pepper and almond salsa 151–2, *153*
herb and feta flatbreads 196
herby olive salsa *20*, 21
herby yogurt 174, *175*
Lebanese herb omelette *98*, 99
lime and herb baked rice *132*, 139
olive oil beans with tomatoes, garlic and herbs *140*, 141
spiced herb sauce 80, *81*
spring onion and herb roti *210*, 211
sumac and barberry herb salad 66, *67*
hibiscus flowers: love tea 244, *245*
hispi cabbage: charred summer cabbage with pomegranate molasses and walnuts *162*, 163
honey
akawi cheese with honey 30, *31*
favourite baklava 218, *219*
four seasons frozen labneh yogurt *224*, 225
lemon and honey potatoes 176, *177*
orange and almond syrup cake 234, *235*
hot chocolate, tahini-spiced 246
hummus and pickled vegetable wrap *78*, 82

I

ice cream, no-churn tahini-espresso 228, *229*

K

ka'ek egg sandwich 82
kale
braised cardamom greens and yogurt *156*, 160, *161*
kale and cheese kataifi bakes *40*, 41
savoury baklava pie 184, *185*
sumac greens 118, *119*
Syrian black-eyed beans and greens 142, *143*
kataifi pastry
kale and cheese kataifi bakes *40*, 41
knafeh 222, *223*
kebabs
Baharat-rubbed mushroom kebabs 80, *81*
dukkah-crusted halloumi skewers *168*, 169
kisses, fudgy salted dark chocolate and sesame 236, *237*
knafeh 222, *223*
koftes, beetroot *96*, 105
koshari, Egyptian 136, *137*
kulcha, spinach *194*, 208

L

labneh
four seasons frozen labneh yogurt *224*, 225
garlic labneh 144, *145*
mint and preserved lime labneh 52, *53*
layered garlic and sesame flatbread 200, *201*
Lebanese cabbage salad 70, *71*
Lebanese chickpea and garlic stew with quick pickled radishes *115*, 122
Lebanese flatbreads 198, *199*
Baharat-spiced *vada pav* with date and tamarind chutney 84, *85*
red cabbage shawarma *88*, 89
squash and walnut *arayes* 79, 83
yogurt-marinated tofu shawarma 90, *91*
Lebanese herb omelette *98*, 99
Lebanese ring bread *204*, 205
lemons
lemon and honey potatoes 176, *177*
quick preserved lemons *48*, 49
lentils
bulgur *mujadara* with nutty red pepper salsa 134, *135*
celebration pie *190*, 191
cumin squash stew with cauliflower and pine nut crumble *114*, 129
Egyptian *koshari* 136, *137*
lentil soup with tamarind and greens 123, *133*
red lentil soup with spiced cauliflower 124, *125*
smoky sumac onion salad 68, *69*
spiced lentil and pine nut curry *47*, 128
lettuce
fresh and crunchy fattoush 60, *61*
sumac and barberry herb salad 66, *67*
limes
black lime and herb tofu 50, *51*
harissa and lime aubergines with crushed chickpeas 174, *175*
lime and herb baked rice *132*, 139

mint and preserved lime labneh 52, *53*
spiced preserved limes 260, *261*
tofu *gondi* dumplings with black lime in tomato sauce 188, *189*
little donut balls 226, *227*
love tea 244, *245*

M

manakish 206, *207*
mango amba sauce *252*, 259
mascarpone, orange blossom apricots with 232, *233*
melons
melon and mint sparkler *241*, 248
melon and yogurt smoothie *242*, 243
mezze
aubergine and tomato mezze 158, *159*
aubergine and yogurt mezze 18, *19*
roasted carrot mezze *13*, 180, *181*
tomato and mint mezze *96*, 173
Middle Eastern noodle soup 126, *127*
milk
aubergine fries 14, *15*
frappe *240*, 244
parsnip and cumin beignets 44
sahlab *240*, 249
sweet *hawaij* coffee 246, *247*
sweet porridge 104
tahini-spiced hot chocolate 246
mint
freekeh tabbouleh *138*, 139
herby olive salsa *20*, 21
herby yogurt 174, *175*
Lebanese herb omelette *98*, 99
melon and mint sparkler *241*, 248
mint and preserved lime labneh 52, *53*
roasted courgette salad with halloumi and mint 182, *183*
sumac and barberry herb salad 66, *67*
tomato and mint mezze *96*, 173
molokhia stew 120, *121*
mozzarella
cheesy sweetcorn nuggets *36*, 37
cheesy za'atar swirls 38, *39*
herb and feta flatbreads 196
knafeh 222, *223*
muhammara, beetroot *12*, 16, *17*
mujadara: bulgur *mujadara* with nutty red pepper salsa 134, *135*
mulberry, orange and sesame seed brittle 228
musakhan, cauliflower 166, *167*
mushrooms: Baharat-rubbed mushroom kebabs 80, *81*

N

no-churn tahini-espresso ice cream 228, *229*
noodles
Egyptian *koshari* 136, *137*
Middle Eastern noodle soup 126, *127*
za'atar cucumber noodle salad 72, *73*
nuggets, cheesy sweetcorn 36, 37
nut-free
akawi cheese with honey 30, *31*
Arabic garlic sauce 258
aubergine fries 14, *15*
Baharat *252*, 254
Baharat-rubbed mushroom kebabs 80, *81*
baked spicy potatoes *177*, 178
beetroot and feta fritters with cumin-dill yogurt 164, *165*
braised runner beans with tomato and cardamom *157*, 179
celebration pie *190*, 191
cheese and herb pastries 32, *33*
coconut cookies *217*, 231
fatayer with spinach and chickpeas 35, *36*
fermented beetroot and turnips 65
fermented red onions *56*, 64
frappe *240*, 244
freekeh tabbouleh *138*, 139
fudgy salted dark chocolate and sesame kisses 236, *237*
garlic tahini sauce 258
harissa and lime aubergines with crushed chickpeas 174, *175*
herb and feta flatbreads 196
hummus and pickled vegetable wrap *78*, 82
layered garlic and sesame flatbread 200, *201*
Lebanese flatbread 198, *199*
Lebanese herb omelette *98*, 99
Lebanese ring bread *204*, 205
lemon and honey potatoes 176, *177*
lentil soup with tamarind and greens 123, *133*
lime and herb baked rice *132*, 139
little donut balls 226, *227*
little rice breakfast buns with harissa eggs 100, *101*
love tea 244, *245*
manakish 206, *207*
melon and mint sparkler *241*, 248
melon and yogurt smoothie *242*, 243
Middle Eastern noodle soup 126, *127*
mint and preserved lime labneh 52, *53*
molokhia stew 120, *121*
mulberry, orange and sesame seed brittle 228
no-churn tahini-espresso ice cream 228, *229*
olive oil beans with tomatoes, garlic and herbs *140*, 141
parsnip and cumin beignets 44
pomegranate juice *241*, 248
pomegranate molasses 256
red cabbage shawarma *88*, 89
red lentil soup with spiced cauliflower 124, *125*
ricotta balls with preserved lemon and Aleppo pepper *48*, 49
roasted courgette salad with halloumi and mint 182, *183*
rose harissa 256
salted yogurt cooler 249
semolina porridge with charred chilli corn 102, *103*
sesame halloumi fries with chilli yogurt 24, *25*
spiced caramelised onion and tofu pastries 45
spiced carrot and chickpea falafel burgers *86*, 87
spiced chickpeas in broth with whipped tahini yogurt *116*, 117
spiced potato cakes 108, *109*
spiced preserved limes 260, *261*
spiced scrambled eggs 106, *107*
spicy roasted chickpeas 14, *15*
summer vegetable grain salad *135*, 150
sweet and sour aubergine sliders 92, *93*
sweet *hawaij* 255
sweet *hawaij* coffee 246, *247*
Syrian black-eyed beans and greens 142, *143*
taboon bread *196*, 209
tahini-spiced hot chocolate 246
tofu *gondi* dumplings with black lime in tomato sauce 188, *189*
Turkish sesame bread 197
watermelon and feta salad 70, *71*
white bean *pkaila* with harissa squash 186, *187*

yogurt-marinated tofu shawarma 90, *91*
zhug 257
nut milk: aubergine fries 14, *15*

O

oils
chilli oil *253*, 257
spiced oil 123, *133*
olive oil beans with tomatoes, garlic and herbs *140*, 141
olives
herby olive salsa *20*, 21
manakish 206, *207*
roasted courgette salad with halloumi and mint 182, *183*
shepherd's salad *73*, 75
spiced herb sauce 80, *81*
watermelon and feta salad 70, *71*
omelette, Lebanese herb *98*, 99
onions
caramelised onions 134, *135*
celebration pie *190*, 191
fermented red onions *56*, 64
pickled onions 90, *91*
pickled red onion 144, *145*
popped beans with pickled red onion and garlic labneh 144, *145*
smoky sumac onion salad 68, *69*
spiced caramelised onion and tofu pastries *29*, 45
orange blossom apricots with mascarpone 232, *233*
oranges
melon and yogurt smoothie *242*, 243
mulberry, orange and sesame seed brittle 228
orange and almond syrup cake 234, *235*

P

panko breadcrumbs
cheesy sweetcorn nuggets *36*, 37
sesame halloumi fries with chilli yogurt 24, *25*
parathas, za'atar 202, *203*
parsley
black lime and herb tofu 50, *51*
braised cardamom greens and yogurt *156*, 160, *161*
freekeh tabbouleh *138*, 139
herb and couscous cake with pepper and almond salsa 151–2, *153*
herb and feta flatbreads 196
Lebanese herb omelette *98*, 99
olive oil beans with tomatoes, garlic and herbs *140*, 141
spiced herb sauce 80, *81*
sumac and barberry herb salad 66, *67*
white bean *pkaila* with harissa squash 186, *187*
zhug 257
parsnip and cumin beignets *28*, 44
pastries
cheese and herb pastries 32, *33*
spiced caramelised onion and tofu pastries *29*, 45
peaches: grilled peaches and toasted sesame shortbread 220, *221*
peas
pea and za'atar falafel 148, *149*
summer vegetable grain salad *135*, 150
sweet and sour aubergine sliders 92, *93*
peppercorns: Baharat *252*, 254
peppers
dukkah-crusted halloumi skewers *168*, 169
nutty red pepper salsa 134, *135*
pepper and almond salsa 151–2, *153*
rose harissa 256
spiced scrambled eggs 106, *107*
Persian toffee brittle *216*, 230
persimmons: four seasons frozen labneh yogurt *224*, 225
pickles
hummus and pickled vegetable wrap *78*, 82
pickled onions 90, *91*
pickled red onion 144, *145*
quick pickled radishes *115*, 122
pies
celebration pie *190*, 191
savoury baklava pie 184, *185*
pine nuts
aubergine and tomato mezze 158, *159*
cheesy za'atar swirls 38, *39*
cumin squash stew with cauliflower and pine nut crumble *114*, 129
roasted carrot mezze 180, *181*
spiced lentil and pine nut curry *47*, 128
pinwheel swirls: cheesy za'atar swirls 38, *39*
pistachios
dukkah 255
favourite baklava 218, *219*
herby olive salsa *20*, 21
knafeh 222, *223*
orange blossom apricots with mascarpone 232, *233*
Persian toffee brittle *216*, 230
pitta breads
courgette and pitta salad 58, *59*
fresh and crunchy fattoush 60, *61*
squash and walnut *arayes* *79*, 83
pkaila: white bean *pkaila* with harissa squash 186, *187*
plums: four seasons frozen labneh yogurt *224*, 225
polenta
aubergine fries 14, *15*
polenta crisps with herby olive salsa *20*, 21
pomegranate
courgette and pitta salad 58, *59*
freekeh tabbouleh *138*, 139
pomegranate juice *241*, 248
tomato and pomegranate salad *67*, 74
pomegranate molasses 256
charred summer cabbage with pomegranate molasses and walnuts *162*, 163
smoky sumac onion salad 68, *69*
sumac and barberry herb salad 66, *67*
sweet and sour aubergine sliders 92, *93*
popped beans with pickled red onion and garlic labneh 144, *145*
porcini mushrooms: tofu *gondi* dumplings with black lime in tomato sauce 188, *189*
porridge
semolina porridge with charred chilli corn 102, *103*
sweet porridge 104
potatoes
Baharat-spiced *vada pav* with date and tamarind chutney 84, *85*
baked spicy potatoes *177*, 178
lemon and honey potatoes 176, *177*
spiced potato cakes 108, *109*
za'atar fries *13*, *22*, 23
preserved lemons *48*, 49
ricotta balls with preserved lemon and Aleppo pepper *48*, 49
preserved limes
mint and preserved lime labneh 52, *53*
spiced preserved limes 260, *261*
puff pastry: cheesy za'atar swirls 38, *39*
pumpkin
golden pumpkin with saffron-butter sauce 170, *171*
white bean *pkaila* with harissa squash 186, *187*

R

radishes
- quick pickled radishes *115*, 122
- summer vegetable grain salad *135*, 150

red kidney beans: tofu *gondi* dumplings with black lime in tomato sauce 188, *189*
rhubarb: four seasons frozen labneh yogurt *224*, 225
rice
- celebration pie *190*, 191
- Egyptian *koshari* 136, *137*
- lime and herb baked rice *132*, 139
- little rice breakfast buns with harissa eggs 100, *101*
- red lentil soup with spiced cauliflower 124, *125*
- tofu *gondi* dumplings with black lime in tomato sauce 188, *189*

ricotta
- celebration pie *190*, 191
- kale and cheese kataifi bakes *40*, 41
- *knafeh* 222, *223*
- ricotta balls with preserved lemon and Aleppo pepper *48*, 49
- smoky sumac onion salad 68, *69*

ring bread, Lebanese *204*, 205
roasted carrot mezze *13*, 180, *181*
rocket (arugula): mint and preserved lime labneh 52, *53*
Romano peppers
- dukkah-crusted halloumi skewers *168*, 169
- nutty red pepper salsa 134, *135*

rose harissa 256
- harissa and lime aubergines with crushed chickpeas 174, *175*
- white bean *pkaila* with harissa squash 186, *187*

rosewater
- grilled peaches and toasted sesame shortbread 220, *221*
- *knafeh* 222, *223*
- little donut balls 226, *227*

roti, spring onion and herb *210*, 211
runner beans: braised runner beans with tomato and cardamom *157*, 179

S

saffron
- love tea 244, *245*
- saffron-butter sauce 170, *171*

sahlab *240*, 249
salads 54–75
- courgette and pitta salad 58, *59*
- cucumber salad 146, *147*
- fermented beetroot and turnips *57*, 65
- fermented red onions *56*, 64
- fresh and crunchy fattoush 60, *61*
- Lebanese cabbage salad 70, *71*
- roasted courgette salad with halloumi and mint 182, *183*
- shepherd's salad *73*, 75
- smoky sumac onion salad 68, *69*
- spiced carrot salad 74, *156*
- sumac and barberry herb salad 66, *67*
- summer vegetable grain salad *135*, 150
- tomato and pomegranate salad *67*, 74
- watermelon and feta salad 70, *71*
- za'atar cucumber noodle salad 72, *73*

salsa
- herby olive salsa *20*, 21
- nutty red pepper salsa 134, *135*
- pepper and almond salsa 151–2, *153*

salted yogurt cooler 249
samosas, spiced tomato and bean 34
sandwiches 74–93
- Baharat-rubbed mushroom kebabs 80, *81*
- Baharat-spiced *vada pav* with date and tamarind chutney 84, *85*
- hummus and pickled vegetable wrap *78*, 82
- *ka'ek* egg sandwich 82
- red cabbage shawarma *88*, 89
- spiced carrot and chickpea falafel burgers *86*, 87
- squash and walnut *arayes* *79*, 83
- sweet and sour aubergine sliders 92, *93*
- yogurt-marinated tofu shawarma 90, *91*

sauces
- Arabic garlic sauce 258
- garlic tahini sauce 258
- mango amba sauce *252*, 259
- saffron-butter sauce 170, *171*
- spiced herb sauce 80, *81*
- tahini sauce *98*, 99
- tomato sauce 188, *189*

savoury baklava pie 184, *185*
semolina (farina)
- polenta crisps *20*, 21
- ricotta balls with preserved lemon and Aleppo pepper *48*, 49
- semolina porridge with charred chilli corn 102, *103*
- sweet porridge 104

sesame seeds
- dukkah 255
- fudgy salted dark chocolate and sesame kisses 236, *237*
- grilled peaches and toasted sesame shortbread 220, *221*
- layered garlic and sesame flatbread 200, *201*
- Lebanese ring bread *204*, 205
- mulberry, orange and sesame seed brittle 228
- pea and za'atar falafel 148, *149*
- savoury baklava pie 184, *185*
- sesame halloumi fries with chilli yogurt 24, *25*
- spinach *kulcha* *194*, 208
- sweet and sour aubergine sliders 92, *93*
- Turkish sesame bread 197
- za'atar 254

shawarma
- red cabbage shawarma *88*, 89
- yogurt-marinated tofu shawarma 90, *91*

shepherd's salad *73*, 75
shortbread, grilled peaches and toasted sesame 220, *221*
skewers, dukkah-crusted halloumi *168*, 169
sliders, sweet and sour aubergine 92, *93*
small plates 26–53
smoky sumac onion salad 68, *69*
smoothies
- creamy almond smoothie *242*, 243
- melon and yogurt smoothie *242*, 243

snacks 10–25
soups
- lentil soup with tamarind and greens 123, *133*
- Middle Eastern noodle soup 126, *127*
- red lentil soup with spiced cauliflower 124, *125*
- spiced chickpeas in broth with whipped tahini yogurt *116*, 117

sparkling water
- melon and mint sparkler *241*, 248
- salted yogurt cooler 249

spices
- Baharat *252*, 254
- baked spicy potatoes *177*, 178
- dukkah 255
- rose harissa 256

spiced caramelised onion and tofu pastries *29*, 45
spiced carrot and chickpea falafel burgers *86*, 87
spiced carrot salad 74, *156*
spiced chickpeas in broth with whipped tahini yogurt *116*, 117
spiced herb sauce 80, *81*
spiced lentil and pine nut curry *47*, 128
spiced potato cakes 108, *109*
spiced preserved limes 260, *261*
spiced scrambled eggs 106, *107*
spiced tomato and bean samosas 34
spicy roasted chickpeas 14, *15*
sweet *hawaij* 255
za'atar 254
zhug 257
spinach
fatayer with spinach and chickpeas 35, *36*
lentil soup with tamarind and greens 123, *133*
manakish 206, *207*
red lentil soup with spiced cauliflower 124, *125*
spinach *borani* with walnuts 172
spinach *kulcha* *194*, 208
sumac greens 118, *119*
white bean *pkaila* with harissa squash 186, *187*
spring greens
savoury baklava pie 184, *185*
Syrian black-eyed beans and greens 142, *143*
spring onion and herb roti *210*, 211
spring rolls, halloumi and za'atar 42, *43*
squash
cumin squash stew with cauliflower and pine nut crumble *114*, 129
squash and walnut *arayes* *79*, 83
white bean *pkaila* with harissa squash 186, *187*
stews
braised chickpeas with sumac greens 118, *119*
cumin squash stew with cauliflower and pine nut crumble *114*, 129
Lebanese chickpea and garlic stew with quick pickled radishes *115*, 122
molokhia stew 120, *121*
spiced chickpeas in broth with whipped tahini yogurt *116*, 117
spiced lentil and pine nut curry *47*, 128
strawberries: four seasons frozen labneh yogurt *224*, 225
sultanas: spiced carrot salad 74, *156*
sumac
braised chickpeas with sumac greens 118, *119*
cauliflower *musakhan* 166, *167*
cucumber salad 146, *147*
grilled corn on the cob with sumac butter *163*
smoky sumac onion salad 68, *69*
sumac and barberry herb salad 66, *67*
za'atar 254
summer cabbage: charred summer cabbage with pomegranate molasses and walnuts *162*, 163
summer vegetable grain salad *135*, 150
sweet and sour aubergine sliders 92, *93*
sweet *hawaij* 255
sweet *hawaij* coffee 246, *247*
sweet porridge 104
sweetcorn: cheesy sweetcorn nuggets *36*, 37
swirls, cheesy za'atar 38, *39*
Swiss chard: red lentil soup with spiced cauliflower 124, *125*
Syrian black-eyed beans and greens 142, *143*
syrup cake, orange and almond 234, *235*

T

tabbouleh, freekeh *138*, 139
taboon bread *196*, 209
tahini
aubergine and tomato mezze 158, *159*
beetroot and feta fritters with cumin-dill yogurt 164, *165*
garlic tahini sauce 258
layered garlic and sesame flatbread 200, *201*
no-churn tahini-espresso ice cream 228, *229*
tahini dressing 72, *73*
tahini sauce *98*, 99
tahini-spiced hot chocolate 246
whipped tahini yogurt *116*, 117
tamarind
date and tamarind chutney 202
lentil soup with tamarind and greens 123, *133*
tea, love 244, *245*
thirty minutes or less
Arabic garlic sauce 258
Baharat *252*, 254
charred summer cabbage with pomegranate molasses and walnuts *162*, 163
chilli oil *253*, 257
creamy almond smoothie *242*, 243
dukkah 255
frappe *240*, 244
fresh and crunchy fattoush 60, *61*
garlic tahini sauce 258
hummus and pickled vegetable wrap *78*, 82
ka'ek egg sandwich 82
Lebanese cabbage salad 70, *71*
Lebanese herb omelette *98*, 99
love tea 244, *245*
melon and yogurt smoothie *242*, 243
molokhia stew 120, *121*
orange blossom apricots with mascarpone 232, *233*
pomegranate juice *241*, 248
roasted courgette salad with halloumi and mint 182, *183*
sahlab *240*, 249
salted yogurt cooler 249
semolina porridge with charred chilli corn 102, *103*
spiced scrambled eggs 106, *107*
sweet *hawaij* 255
sweet *hawaij* coffee 246, *247*
sweet porridge 104
tahini-spiced hot chocolate 246
za'atar 254
za'atar tomato toast 110, *111*
zhug 257
thyme: za'atar 254
toast, za'atar tomato 110, *111*
toffee brittle, Persian *216*, 230
tofu
black lime and herb tofu 50, *51*
spiced caramelised onion and tofu pastries *29*, 45
tofu *gondi* dumplings with black lime in tomato sauce 188, *189*
yogurt-marinated tofu shawarma 90, *91*
tomatoes
aubergine and tomato mezze 158, *159*
braised runner beans with tomato and cardamom *157*, 179
celebration pie *190*, 191
courgette and pitta salad 58, *59*
cucumber salad 146, *147*
Egyptian *koshari* 136, *137*
fresh and crunchy fattoush 60, *61*
Lebanese cabbage salad 70, *71*
manakish 206, *207*
olive oil beans with tomatoes, garlic and herbs *140*, 141

pepper and almond salsa 151–2, *153*
shepherd's salad *73*, 75
spiced lentil and pine nut curry *47*, 128
spiced scrambled eggs 106, *107*
spiced tomato and bean samosas 34
tofu *gondi* dumplings with black lime in tomato sauce 188, *189*
tomato and mint mezze *96*, 173
tomato and pomegranate salad *67*, 74
za'atar tomato toast 110, *111*
tortillas: hummus and pickled vegetable wrap *78*, 82
Turkish green peppers: spiced scrambled eggs 106, *107*
Turkish sesame bread 197
turnips, fermented beetroot and *57*, 65

V

vada pav: Baharat-spiced *vada pav* with date and tamarind chutney 84, *85*
vegan
Arabic garlic sauce 258
Baharat *252*, 254
baked spicy potatoes *177*, 178
beetroot koftes *96*, 105
black lime and herb tofu 50, *51*
braised runner beans with tomato and cardamom *157*, 179
bulgur *mujadara* with nutty red pepper salsa 134, *135*
chickpea pancakes 46, *47*
chilli oil *253*, 257
creamy almond smoothie *242*, 243
cumin squash stew with cauliflower and pine nut crumble *114*, 129
dukkah 255
fermented beetroot and turnips 65
fermented red cabbage *62*, 63
fermented red onions *56*, 64
freekeh tabbouleh *138*, 139
fresh and crunchy fattoush 60, *61*
hummus and pickled vegetable wrap *78*, 82
layered garlic and sesame flatbread 200, *201*
Lebanese cabbage salad 70, *71*
Lebanese flatbread 198, *199*
lime and herb baked rice *132*, 139
manakish 206, *207*
mango amba sauce 259
melon and mint sparkler *241*, 248
molokhia stew 120, *121*
mulberry, orange and sesame seed brittle 228
pea and za'atar falafel 148, *149*
polenta crisps with herby olive salsa *20*, 21
pomegranate juice *241*, 248
pomegranate molasses 256
quick falafel 146, *147*
red lentil soup with spiced cauliflower 124, *125*
rose harissa 256
shepherd's salad *73*, 75
spiced carrot salad 74, *156*
spiced lentil and pine nut curry *47*, 128
spiced preserved limes 260, *261*
spiced tomato and bean samosas 34
spicy roasted chickpeas 14, *15*
summer vegetable grain salad *135*, 150
sweet *hawaij* 255
Syrian black-eyed beans and greens 142, *143*
taboon bread *196*, 209
tofu *gondi* dumplings with black lime in tomato sauce 188, *189*
tomato and pomegranate salad *67*, 74
Turkish sesame bread 197
white bean *pkaila* with harissa squash 186, *187*
za'atar 254
za'atar fries *13*, *22*, 23
za'atar tomato toast 110, *111*
zhug 257
vegetables 154–91
hummus and pickled vegetable wrap *78*, 82
summer vegetable grain salad *135*, 150
see also individual types of vegetable
vermicelli
Egyptian *koshari* 136, *137*
Middle Eastern noodle soup 126, *127*

walnuts
beetroot *muhammara* *12*, 16, *17*
charred summer cabbage with pomegranate molasses and walnuts *162*, 163
garlic and walnut dip *12*, 16, *17*
nutty red pepper salsa 134, *135*
savoury baklava pie 184, *185*
spiced tomato and bean samosas 34
spinach *borani* with walnuts 172
squash and walnut *arayes* *79*, 83
watermelon and feta salad 70, *71*
white bean *pkaila* with harissa squash 186, *187*
wonton wrappers: halloumi and za'atar spring rolls 42, *43*
wraps, hummus and pickled vegetable *78*, 82

yogurt
aubergine and yogurt mezze 18, *19*
braised cardamom greens and yogurt *156*, 160, *161*
chilli yogurt 24, *25*
cumin-dill yogurt 164, *165*
fatayer with spinach and chickpeas 35, *36*
four seasons frozen labneh yogurt *224*, 225
garlic labneh 144, *145*
garlic yogurt 44
harissa and lime aubergines with crushed chickpeas 174, *175*
herb and couscous cake with pepper and almond salsa 151–2, *153*
melon and yogurt smoothie *242*, 243
mint and preserved lime labneh 52, *53*
salted yogurt cooler 249
spinach *borani* with walnuts 172
spinach *kulcha* *194*, 208
whipped tahini yogurt *116*, 117
yogurt-marinated tofu shawarma 90, *91*

Z

za'atar 254
braised cardamom greens and yogurt *156*, 160, *161*
cheesy za'atar swirls 38, *39*
chickpea pancakes 46, *47*
fresh and crunchy fattoush 60, *61*
halloumi and za'atar spring rolls 42, *43*
manakish 206, *207*
pea and za'atar falafel 148, *149*
spinach *kulcha* *194*, 208
za'atar cucumber noodle salad 72, *73*
za'atar fries *13*, *22*, 23
za'atar garlic bread 212, *213*
za'atar parathas 202, *203*
za'atar tomato toast 110, *111*
zhug 257

Phaidon Press Limited
2 Cooperage Yard
London E15 2QR

Phaidon Press Inc.
111 Broadway
New York, NY 10006

phaidon.com

First published 2024

ISBN 978 1 83866 764 1

A CIP catalogue record for this book is available from the British Library and the Library of Congress.

Commissioning Editor: Ellie Smith
Project Editor: Rachel Malig
Designer: Evi-O.Studio | Evi O.
Typesetting: Evi-O.Studio | Matt Crawford
Production Controller: Gif Jittiwutikarn
Photography: Haarala Hamilton
Styling: Penelope Parker

Printed in China.

The publisher would like to thank: Vanessa Bird, Emi Chiba, Julia Hasting, Susan Le, Michelle Meade, João Mota, Evi O., Pamela Sarly, Anna Shepherd, Tracey Smith, Kathy Steer and Lucie Ware for their contribution to the book.

RECIPE NOTES

- Butter should always be unsalted, unless otherwise specified.
- All herbs are fresh, unless otherwise specified.
- Eggs are medium (US large) unless otherwise specified.
- Individual vegetables and fruits, such as onions and apples, are assumed to be medium, unless otherwise specified.
- All milk is whole (3% fat), homogenised and lightly pasteurized, unless otherwise specified.
- All salt is fine sea salt, unless otherwise specified.
- True Parmesan cheese uses rennet and is therefore not vegetarian. When a recipe lists Parmesan-style cheese, use a hard cheese with a similar flavour profile that uses vegetarian rennet. There are many available on the market.
- Always check labels of cheeses and other pre-prepared ingredients and choose a brand that is vegetarian.
- Exercise a high level of caution when following recipes involving any potentially hazardous activity, including the use of high temperatures, open flames and when deep-frying. In particular, when deep-frying add food carefully to avoid splashing, wear long sleeves and never leave the pan unattended.
- Cooking times are for guidance only. If using a fan (convection) oven, follow the manufacturer's instructions concerning the oven temperatures.
- All herbs, shoots, flowers and leaves should be picked fresh from a clean source. Do exercise caution when foraging for ingredients, which should only be eaten if an expert has deemed them safe to eat. In particular, do not gather wild mushrooms yourself before seeking the advice of an expert who has confirmed their suitability for human consumption. As some species of mushrooms have been known to cause allergic reaction and illness, do take extra care when cooking and eating mushrooms and do seek immediate medical help if you experience a reaction after preparing or eating them.
- Exercise caution when making fermented products, ensuring all equipment is spotlessly clean, and seek expert advice if in any doubt.
- When no quantity is specified, for example of oils, salts and herbs used for finishing dishes, quantities are discretionary and flexible.
- All spoon and cup measurements are level, unless otherwise stated. 1 teaspoon = 5 ml; 1 tablespoon = 15 ml. Australian standard tablespoons are 20 ml, so Australian readers are advised to use 3 teaspoons in place of 1 tablespoon when measuring small quantities.
- Cup, metric and imperial measurements are used in this book. Follow one set of measurements throughout, not a mixture, as they are interchangeable.

ABOUT THE AUTHOR

Lebanese Salma Hage, from Mazarat Tiffah (Apple Hamlet) in the mountains of the Kadisha Valley in north Lebanon, has more than 50 years of experience of family cooking. She learned to cook from her mother, mother-in-law, and sisters-in-law, and spent many years working as a professional cook. This is her fifth book, after *The Lebanese Kitchen*, the James Beard Award-winning *The Middle Eastern Vegetarian Cookbook*, *The Mezze Cookbook* and *Middle Eastern Sweets*.